Transcendent Woman

Transcendent Woman

**MARGARET FULLER'S ART
AND ACHIEVEMENT**

DAVID M. ROBINSON

University of Massachusetts Press
AMHERST AND BOSTON

Copyright © 2025 by University of Massachusetts Press
All rights reserved

ISBN 978-1-62534-878-4 (paper); 879-1 (hardcover)

Designed by Jen Jackowitz
Set in Adobe Jenson Pro
Printed and bound by Books International, Inc.

Cover design by adam b. bohannon
Cover photo by John Plumbe, Jr. *Portrait of Margaret Fuller*,
1846, sixth-plate daguerreotype. National Portrait Gallery. CC0 1.0.

Library of Congress Cataloging-in-Publication Data
A catalog record for this book is available from the Library of Congress.

British Library Cataloguing-in-Publication Data
A catalog record for this book is available from the British Library.

CONTENTS

INTRODUCTION
1

CHAPTER 1
"True Disciples of the Nineteenth Century"
3

CHAPTER 2
The "Flame-like" Soul
29

CHAPTER 3
"The Intelligent Freedom of the Universe"
55

CHAPTER 4
Vital Energy
85

CHAPTER 5
Young Europe and Its Democracy
108

NOTES   137

INDEX   149

Transcendent Woman

INTRODUCTION

This book will follow the intellectual development and influence of Margaret Fuller, an originating voice in the women's movement in both the United States and Europe. Her *Woman in the Nineteenth Century* was published in 1845, just before she became an international journalist. Innovative and controversial, Fuller was a key figure in transcendentalism, America's first philosophical revolution. Now a renowned figure in the study of American literature and women's history, Fuller—along with her work and accomplishment—had gradually fallen into neglect in the later nineteenth century and most of the twentieth. The rise of the women's rights movement in the 1960s and 1970s brought a renewed interest in women authors and in the literature and principles of the progressive transcendentalists Ralph Waldo Emerson and Henry David Thoreau. By the 1980s, the analysis of Fuller's central works, particularly *Woman in the Nineteenth Century*, had established a substantial impact on the literary and cultural history of the United States.

A series of biographies and critical essays beginning in the 1970s have been central to Fuller's rediscovery as an eminent figure in American culture. Bell Gale Chevigny's "open form" biography and reader *The Woman and the Myth* (1976) opened Fuller to a decade of readers, with numerous books and essays furthering the significance of Fuller's legacy. Charles

Capper's two vast and brilliant volumes of *Margaret Fuller: An American Romantic Life* (1992, 2007), seemed to be the defining work for Fuller's biography, but six years later Megan Marshall won the Pulitzer Prize with her superb and deeply meaningful *Margaret Fuller: A New American Life*.

Grounding these biographies were New England's abundant libraries at Harvard and the Massachusetts Historical Society, whose holdings included an enormous collection of handwritten letters, journals, and manuscripts of most of the authors related to transcendentalism, including Fuller. Many of her crucial works had been preserved, including her sizable correspondence. Researchers arose to edit and publish Fuller's valued writings in the 1970s, headed by the erudite and energetic scholar Joel Myerson. Critical analyses, historical discoveries, and editions of essays continued to build Fuller's repute. Important advances were made by Robert N. Hudspeth's six-volume edition of Fuller's letters (1983–1994), a compendium of her thoughts and inspirations. That scholarly feat was followed by Larry J. Reynolds and Susan Belasco's 1991 recovery of Fuller's European dispatches to the *New-York Tribune*, a guide to the last year of her life, and confirmation of her compelling love of the idea of democracy.

This book describes the most important steps in Fuller's thoughts, her clashes with her adversaries, her misery, and her ecstasy. Fuller can best be understood through her "art"—and her art was her craft with the word. Taught to master reading and writing as a child, Fuller lived in the world of conversation and the composing and receiving of letters. As she cultivated her skills of discourse, she began to see it as her life's mission: she must undertake to rescue all constrained women and men from their bondage. Her correspondence, her publications, her public performances of Conversations for women, the book *Woman in the Nineteenth Century*, and her journalistic dispatches from Europe continue to speak to us. This volume is the account of her mission.

CHAPTER 1
"True Disciples of the Nineteenth Century"

Vibratiuncles and Reason

In the fall of 1831, Margaret Fuller and James Freeman Clarke agreed that they would undertake together the study of German. This momentous compact would alter their patterns of thinking and mark a departure in the course of their lives, with especially profound implications for Fuller. Germany would become for her and many others with literary or theological aspirations the undiscovered land of philosophical innovation and imaginative freedom. Ralph Waldo Emerson called it "my Germany of mystic philosophy and dreams" in his first book, *Nature*.[1] Its writers and philosophers promised to take them far beyond the doctrinal confines of New England religion and the pedestrian limitations of British philosophy. To master German was to unlock the doors that seemed to be closed before them as spiritual searchers.

At twenty-one, they were both dissatisfied and restless; they craved the newness.

Fuller, who had been drilled in Latin by her demanding father from the age of four, grasped the German language with extraordinary quickness. Beginning her studies early in 1832, she was reading fluently in the key works of modern German literature within three months. Clarke, a solid linguist himself, was amazed. "Within the year, she had read Goethe's

Faust, Tasso, Iphigenia, Hermann and Dorothea, Elective Affinities and Memoirs; Tieck's William Lovel, Prince Zerbino, and other works; Körner, Novalis, and something of Richter; all of Schiller's principal dramas, and his lyric poetry." While Clarke had been immersed in many of the same texts and had found in them powerful support for new departures in his own spiritual path, he was deeply impressed with both the speed and depth with which Fuller had taken command of modern German literature. "Almost every evening I saw her, and heard an account of her studies. Her mind opened under this influence, as the apple-blossom at the end of a warm week in May."[2]

Fuller and Clarke had met in Cambridge during Clarke's undergraduate studies at Harvard, brought together through a network of mutual friends and their shared literary interests. They were each somewhat adrift, undergoing both family disruptions and periodic romantic distresses. Their friendship developed during an intellectually expansive but conflict-ridden period at Harvard and in the Boston area churches, which included a dramatic liberalization of theological doctrines and religious sensibilities and a greater openness to the art and ideas that were having a transformative impact on Europe. Though excluded, as a woman, from Harvard and from a career in the ministry, Fuller was nevertheless a beneficiary of the newness that was opening up Cambridge and Boston. She found friends among Harvard's students and its liberal-minded Unitarian clergy, absorbed the expansive religious atmosphere, and benefited from the city's rudimentary but quickly developing literary culture. By the time she met Clarke, she was in charge of her own self-education and seemed as unswerving as her rigorous father in her intellectual demands of herself. Fuller's prowess and wide reading impressed, and sometimes alarmed, most of those she met. "She had a dangerous reputation for satire, in addition to her great scholarship," Emerson later wrote (*Memoirs* 1:202).

Attracted by their shared need for companionship and intellectual challenge, Fuller and Clarke developed a close friendship, founded in part on their allegiance to the "newness," the currents of romanticism and religious liberalism that were reaching America. We are "true disciples of the nineteenth century," Fuller wrote to him in an 1830 letter.[3] In the religious sphere, this new sensibility first took the name of Unitarianism, as the

Boston churches founded by Puritan Calvinists gradually declared themselves independent in the 1820s and 1830s. Clarke was the first of several Unitarian ministers who became close friends and intellectual confidants of Fuller, including Frederic Henry Hedge, Ralph Waldo Emerson, and William Henry Channing. Though shaped by Unitarian culture, Fuller and her friends came to find the institutionalized, moderately affluent, and carefully conventional Boston-Cambridge version of it inadequate as a spiritual resource. Their attempts to intensify its spiritual ardor and expand its intellectual boundaries developed into a countermovement that came to be known as "transcendentalism."[4]

Unitarian beginnings in New England can be traced well into the eighteenth century, as the Puritan churches in the Boston area began to question Calvinist doctrines such as innate human depravity and salvation of the predetermined elect. Minister by minister and church by church, the rejection of Calvinist orthodoxy advanced, and by the 1820s the liberals coalesced into a separate religious denomination and claimed the name "unitarian," largely controlling Harvard, and encompassing most of the original Puritan churches in the Boston area. At its core, Unitarianism was a new conception of human nature, which held that men and women were not innately depraved, nor were they effortlessly moral or inevitably spiritual. Unitarians affirmed human potential, not absolute human goodness. Life was a period of trial in which the tested soul might learn to claim and develop its spiritual potential.

The Boston Unitarianism of the 1820s and 1830s presented Fuller, Clarke, and their like-minded friends with two rather different faces. The eloquent and spiritual William Ellery Channing was an inspiring preacher, generally regarded as the central voice of New England Unitarianism. Channing's contemporary Andrews Norton was a Harvard biblical scholar whose research attempted to anchor liberal Christianity in biblical certainty. Channing had been a trenchant critic of Calvinism, skewering its signature dogma of predestination as morally offensive and a slander on the benevolent character of God. He defined religion as a continual effort to attain "Likeness to God," as his most characteristic sermon expressed it.[5] Norton, too, had been a strong critic of Calvinism, who had turned his intellectual focus toward the challenge of German biblical criticism, whose historicist approach to the Bible put claims to its absolute authority into question.

Channing remained the central figure of the emerging Unitarian denomination, but Norton became, for many younger Unitarians, the spokesman for a lost theological cause, and the symbol of a threatening religious and academic establishment that had lost its vitality and its intellectual authority. The battle that Channing and Norton fought against Calvinism would not be taken up by the next generation, for whom doctrines like election to grace were a superstition of the distant past. Norton shared Channing's aversion to Calvinism, but he connected religious truth with verifiable evidence of the miraculous and supernatural—the belief that reliable witnesses had directly observed the acts of Jesus, and that their accounts had been preserved for posterity as proof of his divine character and mission. Channing's theology was internal and spiritual; Norton's was external and empirical. Norton's conception of the empirical foundation of religious truth was utterly repellent to the emerging transcendentalists, all of whom were able to testify to some form of intuitive or self-originating experience that revealed truths beyond the material and confirmed a higher or transcendent mode of perception. These were often moments of extreme emotional intensity or of great elation, remembered as life-transforming events, or points at which the soul's development took a new direction. Clarke's and Fuller's accounts of their own shaping spiritual moments will provide a firmer grip on the notoriously slippery label transcendentalist.

Clarke's grandfather James Freeman was the first American cleric to identify himself as a Unitarian, serving for over four decades as minister of King's Chapel in Boston. Clarke directly connected his religious turning point with his grandfather's ministerial prominence, embodied by the library that represented his philosophical attainment and legacy. "The books of Locke, Priestly, Hartley, and Belsham were in my grandfather Freeman's library," Clarke recalled, "and the polemic of Locke against innate ideas was one of my earliest philosophical lessons." Locke had rejected the notion of "innate ideas" and argued instead that ideas were the products of sense impressions originating in the mind's response to external stimuli. Lockean theory placed the mind in a passive position and famously characterized it as the blank pages that the senses filled with their impressions. Clarke balked at this depiction of the mind as inert, and of thinking as a kind of instinctive response. It seemed to reduce vital perceptual and imaginative processes to a robotic functionality. "Something within me revolted at all such attempts to explain soul out of sense, deducing mind from matter, or tracing the origin of ideas to nerves, vibrations, and vibratiuncles," Clarke wrote.[6] The curious term "vibratiuncles," which he remembered with derision from his youthful reading, was coined by the English philosopher and physician David Hartley, who viewed the material as energetic and the mind as passive.[7] Clarke was so distressed by this conception of the mind that he considered abandoning philosophical theology altogether, a resolve that lasted, he recalled, "until Coleridge showed me from Kant that though knowledge begins *with* experience it does not come *from* experience." Coleridge fulfilled, he said, "my longing for a higher philosophy," and "then I discovered that I was born a transcendentalist" (JFC 39). This was, for Clarke, a self-defining moment; he speaks not of a *change* of self but of a *discovery* of self, an affirmation of the identity that he felt he had always already possessed but had been unable to name or realize fully.

Coleridge's contribution to budding transcendentalists like Clarke was his formulation of the Kantian distinction between two forms of thought, a lower "Understanding" that was sense-bound and empirical in its operations, and a higher "Reason" that was active and creative in its perceptual capacities.[8] The "Understanding," which depends "on the representations of the Senses," Coleridge argued, is different "in *kind*" from "the speculative Reason," a dynamic power through which universal laws can be drawn from the representations of experience that the Understanding provides. Reason thus represented the mind's access to both creative power and holistic vision.[9] This conception of an elevated perceptive power affirmed trans-rational forms of thinking such as intuition, aesthetic appreciation, and spiritual experience. In Reason, artistic urges and spiritual aspirations converged, making the reading and writing of literature a sacred act. Emerson came to regard assent to the concept of Reason as a kind of spiritual litmus test. "Various terms are employed to indicate the counteraction of the Reason & the Understanding, with more or less precision according to the cultivation of the speaker," he wrote in his journal. "A clear perception of it, is the key to all theology, and a theory of human life."[10] Allegiance to "Reason," as defined in this romantic sense, thus became a defining mark of transcendentalist revolt.

Clarke's elated witness to the transformative power of Coleridge's description of a mental faculty operating beyond the limitations of physical sensation suggests the power of this idea, and it was further magnified by Frederic Henry Hedge's perceptive and influential essay of 1833, "Coleridge's Literary Character," one of the founding documents of the transcendentalist movement.[11] Hedge praised James Marsh's "valuable dissertation" on Coleridge's *Aids to Reflection*, but offered a somewhat stringent assessment of Coleridge himself, a potentially great author, he felt, whose literary achievement had been spoiled by an inability to attain an organic unity in his larger projects. That flaw had been amplified by the diversion of his energies to inconsequential reviews. Hedge distinguished his critique, however, from those that resisted Coleridge for his "obscurity," a charge he recognized as code for anti-transcendentalism. "The greater part of this alleged obscurity exists in the mind of the reader," Hedge stated, noting a lamentable lack of diligence among modern readers. "Whatever taxes the mind, instead of exciting it, is deemed a burthen. A hard word scares us; a proposition, which does not explain itself at first glance, troubles us; whatever is *supersensual* and cannot be made plain by images addressed to the senses, is denounced as obscure, or beckoned away as mystical and extravagant" (Hedge 117). Turning the "obscurity" argument into an indictment of indolence, Hedge then offered a trenchant delineation of "German metaphysics," the Kantian idealism that had liberated Clarke, arguing that its basis was "the interior consciousness, distinguished from the common consciousness, by its being an active and not a passive state." Such consciousness "is a free intuition, and can only be attained by a vigorous effort of the will" (Hedge 119).

Hedge's exposition of an inner awareness would give intellectual weight and confirmation to the process of liberating self-discovery that Clarke was describing to Fuller in their correspondence. He wrote to her in 1830 to relate his experiments in recording and analyzing his dreams, attempting to use them to gain a deeper understanding of his own inner perception. Dreams, he conjectured, were the working of "the *Imagination*, freed from the bondage of reality, of the senses, of waking perceptions, and riding unrestrainedly in the limitless world of its own creation." For Clarke, the state of sleep allowed the imagination, something close to what Coleridge would call the Reason, to reassert its essential control over the mind, freed from the material world and its constraints. "This is a great purpose of sleep," he wrote, "and not, as Hartley supposes, merely to prevent our associations from becoming so cemented together that we could not disjoin them by any act of the will, which would be madness." The imagination, during sleep, is fortifying itself, "gathering strength to support the soul and maintain its activity against the otherwise crushing influence of continued impressions from an outward world. The imagination is thus the sign of an inner power, actively shaping ideas and perceptions, and giving the mind an active rather than a passive character." For oh, dear Margaret, we are not the slaves of association. It is not true, that debasing theory, that our thoughts are brought into our minds by certain laws, fixed and invariable as the laws of the material world."[12]

For Clarke, the stakes of this philosophical debate over the nature of the mind were high: to be free or to be a slave; to command inner resources and capabilities or to be powerless and inert before an onslaught of controlling stimuli. A theory of life or thought in which one simply responded mechanistically to external stimuli seemed a living death. That he would pour out his philosophical ideas with so much passion to Fuller is a testament to the emotional openness and shared intellectual aspiration that marked their correspondence in an era in which the letter was a powerful instrument of friendship, communication, and original thought. Clarke had written to her on March 27, 1830, in what appears to be a continuation of a recent conversation in which she had expressed reservations about entering a fully open and reciprocal exchange. "You cannot expect from me that which you do not return," Clarke insisted. If he is, in other words, to pour out confidential confessions to her, she must also be open with him. "It is only when I know that those to whom I write or speak are ready to give me an equal store of treasured emotions, that the ice-bars break from the depths of my nature, and the hidden fountains well upwards" (*JFC Fuller* 11).

In response Fuller alluded to the failure of a previous attempt at such a friendship with another man, and also reminded Clarke of a failed earlier attempt to open such a relationship with him. "I cannot promise you any limitless confidence," she explained, "but I *can* promise no timid caution, no haughty dread shall prevent my telling you the truth of my thoughts on any subject we may have in common. Will it satisfy you? Oh let it; suffer me to know you" (*FL* 6:164–65). There is emotional reserve here, a setting of limits, but also a desire for a largely proscribed freedom of self-expression and interchange. There is an undercurrent of emotional, even erotic attraction in this interchange, but more importantly, there is an opportunity for intimate intellectual dialogue. A philosophy that cannot find expression is lost. Fuller and Clarke saw in each other a channel for the expression of ideas that might otherwise wither. In the quickening but still thin and constricted New England atmosphere, that was crucially important. The transcendentalists faced a world that seemed to them hostile not simply to new ideas but to self-expression and sincere friendship. A desire for honest expression and open conversation, exemplified in the exchanges between Fuller and Clarke, permeated the public and private writings of the group. For Fuller and Clarke, letters were crucial sources of mutual stimulus and encouragement at a time when each of them seemed to be searching for fresher intellectual and emotional air. "Electrify my stupor with your generosity," Clarke wrote, begging for a letter from Fuller. "Write me a letter containing any of those states of feeling which you have so often felt and never forgotten—give me 'the mood in life' or any other mood" (*JFC Fuller* 13). If Clarke needed the stimulus of fresh ideas, Fuller needed a confidant like Clarke to whom she could express herself in open dialogue in a culture that she found stifling. "Let us be free in friendship," she wrote to Clarke. "The world confines us close enough in all else" (*FL* 6:211). It is fitting, then, that Clarke recalled Coleridge's collection of essays *The Friend* as one of the texts that liberated him from the slavery of Locke and Hartley. Coleridge insisted on the social rather than the solitary nature of learning, arguing in *The Friend* that "his lot is happy who owes this protection to friendship: who has found in a friend the watchful guardian of his mind. He will not be deluded, having that light to guide: he will not slumber with that voice to inspire; he will not be desponding or dejected, with that bosom to lean on."[13] Intellectual growth is, in certain crucial respects, a shared or communal affair, Coleridge believed. Fuller and Clarke were confirming this idea and finding vital encouragement in their shared restlessness. Friendship, expressed through vivid letters and earnest conversation, remained essential in the fabric of the transcendentalist movement.

"Conversation is my natural element"

Fuller's sensibility included a profoundly religious, even mystical element: she harbored continual doubts about the Christian revelation, even in its more liberal Unitarian version. She had from childhood been steeped in the Roman and Greek classics and had been a serious, wide-ranging reader from childhood. She thus seemed to take an instinctively critical and historical view of Christianity and to be quite open in sharing her periodic doubts with her friends. When George Davis, her first significant romantic interest, queried her about her religious views in early 1830, the nineteen- year-old Fuller answered with the frankness that was one of her distinguishing traits. "I have not formed an opinion" on religion, she told him, linking her indecision to a sense of strength and personal integrity. "Loving or feeble natures need a positive religion, a visible refuge, a protection, as much in the passionate season of youth as in those stages nearer to the grave. But mine is not such" (*FL* 1:158). Fuller wanted to make it clear that she was a strong soul who sought no refuge in a sentimental religion. But as she explained herself to Davis, in a somewhat self-dramatizing way, she drew a picture of one whose intellectual courage also entailed a certain proud stoicism. "My pride is superior to any feelings I have yet experienced: my affection is strong admiration, not the necessity of giving or receiving assistance or sympathy," she wrote. "When disappointed I do not ask or wish consolation,—I wish to know and feel my pain, to investigate its nature and source; I will not have my thoughts diverted, or my feelings soothed; 't is therefore that my young life is singularly barren of illusions." She may have been enacting a brave role here for Davis's benefit, but her theatrics were grounded in a genuinely noncommittal attitude toward Christianity. "I believe in a God, a Beauty and Perfection to which I am to strive all my life for assimilation. From these two articles of belief, I draw the rules by which I strive to regulate my life" (FL 1:158–59). Her brushing Christianity aside as unsuited for her is perhaps bolder than any direct declaration of rational disbelief. It certainly suggests her determination to make such external decisions and allegiances on her own terms, and to resist any pressure to conform her own to any external norms.

Such insistent self-reliance did not mean that Fuller was unconcerned with religious questions. In fact, they seemed to grow in importance during her twenties, taking a uniquely personal formulation in her thought. We can find one barometer of her outlook in two letters to Hedge, written several years after her interchange with Davis. A Unitarian minister in West Cambridge in the early 1830s when Clarke and Fuller were reading German together, Hedge was a lifeline to Fuller after her family moved from Cambridge to rural Groton. He had been educated in a German gymnasium before completing Harvard College and Divinity School. His German was fluent and his understanding of modern German literature deep. Fuller praised his "daring yet realizing mind" (FL 6:163), seeing him as a man of great learning and of balanced judgment. She confided her religious searching to him, writing of her plans "to examine thoroughly as far as my time and abilities permit the evidences of the Christian religion," in hope that such study would allow her "to adopt the religion as a matter of taste." She wryly confessed, however, certain obstacles to the plan. "But I meet with Infidels very often, two or three of my particular friends are Deists—their arguments and several distressing skeptical notions of my own are haunting me forever—I *must* satisfy myself and having once begun I shall go as far as I can" (FL 1:213). In a letter, however, she described for Hedge her utter inability to read the influential biblical scholar Johann Gottfried Eichhorn, whose work Hedge revered, explaining that his detailed textual analysis was not the kind of reassurance she sought. "I wish, if possible, to be a Christian and to become so not in sickness and adversity but in health and in the full possession of my reasoning powers." She had felt herself a Christian, she admitted, only during "times of excitement," always finding that "skepticism returns" (*FL* 1:223). Her doubt, as she explained it to Hedge, was of the sort that might well qualify her as a deist. "I have no confidence in God as a Father." She lacked, in other words, a belief in "an over-ruling Providence" that could provide her with a clearer understanding of "many things which seem dark and hateful to me now" (*FL* 1:224).

Fuller's inability to believe in "God as a Father" should not obscure her ongoing attempts to forge a spirituality beyond the doctrinal and conceptual sphere of Christianity. She was in sympathy with the holistic vision of the cosmos that was an important element of transcendentalist thinking. But she was moved by literature, not theology, and responded more directly and more passionately to what Clarke termed "the wild bugle call of Thomas Carlyle" (*Memoirs* 1:114), who championed the German romantics with an extraordinary stylistic ardor. That her allegiance to the "new views" had a somewhat different grounding sheds light on her own course of self-development and emphasizes the wide range of sensibilities among the transcendentalists. As Emerson would later observe, there was no "concert of doctrinaires to establish certain opinions, & inaugurate some movement in literature, philosophy, & religion" (*JMN* 16:21–22). Fuller was not by temperament drawn to metaphysical system building or the intricacies of epistemological theory. To discuss philosophy or theology with Clarke was always, for Fuller, to be reminded that he was launching a professional career and that she was not, a fact that reinforced her innate reservations about abstract metaphysics and epistemology. "Happy you, in these ideas which give you a tendency to optimism," she wrote to Clarke. "May you become a proselyte to that consoling faith. I shall never be able to follow you, but shall look after you with longing eyes" (*FL* 1:179).

Clarke's witness to the power of Coleridge's exposition of Kant, as we have seen, provided one instance of the transformative power of this new philosophy. Another was Fuller's discovery of the German poet and philosopher Novalis in 1832. The agent of the revelation was Thomas Carlyle, whose brilliant overview of Novalis as a figure of deep sorrow and almost beatific glory profoundly moved Fuller.[14] "I have not got anybody to speak to that does not talk commonplace," Fuller excitedly wrote to Clarke in 1832. "And I wish to talk about such an uncommon person—About Novalis!" (*FL* 6:187). Fuller had reason for excitement not only in the moving life story and strikingly original works of Novalis but also in Carlyle's dazzling presentation of him as the quintessential transcendentalist poet-philosopher. Carlyle opened the full panoply of German philosophy and romantic literature to English readers in a series of critical reviews in the 1820s and early 1830s. These had a galvanizing impact on the transcendentalists. He conveyed enormous amounts of information on German authors, books, and ideas to a New England readership hungry for the new, and astonished them with arresting prose, "passionate, urgent, full of humor and outrage," as Barbara Packer writes.[15] By no means a theologian or systematic philosopher in the Germanic sense, Carlyle nevertheless understood the importance of Kant's Copernican Revolution in philosophy and recognized its significance to the flowering of German romanticism. For Carlyle, the liveliness of German writing accentuated the moribund state of British literature and culture. His mission was to transmit this intellectual energy to his readers with the conviction that they were witnesses to, and might indeed become a part of, a world-changing transformation of thought.

Carlyle presented Novalis as the modern philosopher-poet in whom beauty and spirituality were one and the same, and thereby helped Fuller bind together the worlds she had felt to be not just separate but perhaps in conflict. He recognized Novalis's originality and an element of deep spirituality. "Novalis was a Mystic, or had an affinity with Mysticism," he wrote. He possessed a "spiritual condition" beyond the power of words to describe, "like pure Light, colourless, formless, infinite" (CNovalis 113). Novalis was thus an idealist of a different sort within the larger tradition of Kant. Through Novalis, Carlyle was able to mount a sustained attack on the Scottish common sense philosophers who were the chief conservators of Locke in the early nineteenth century. "The Idealist again boasts that his Philosophy is Transcendental, that is, 'ascending beyond the senses,'" wrote Carlyle. "Matter has an existence, but only as a Phenomenon" (CNovalis 115). Emerson would later reiterate this central transcendentalist principle in more oracular terms. "Idealism saith: Matter is a phenomenon, not a substance" (*CW* 1:37).

"Sometimes," Carlyle wrote, Novalis "seems to represent the Primeval essence of Being as Love" (*CNovalis* 119). The significance of the bond between love and the mystical would by no means have been lost on Fuller. She was little moved by rigorous theological systems and philosophical absolutes. "The use of metaphysics," she drily reminded Clarke, should be restricted to "a moderate portion, taken at stated intervals" (*FL* 1:179). Clarke, however, had shown something remarkable. "I felt very *new* about Novalis—'the good Novalis,' as you call him after Mr. Carlyle. He is indeed good, most enlightened, yet most pure; every link of his experience framed— no, beaten—from tried gold" (*FL* 1:178). Her predisposition was moving toward an aesthetic way of thought, one that emerged from literary texts or works of art, as an alternative to the totalized metaphysical systems of Kant or Fichte. With Carlyle's help, Fuller found this poetic philosophy in Novalis. A month after she had encountered Novalis, she responded to one of Clarke's sermons, making it clear that she was drawn to a quite different philosophical path. "I have taken no pains to think, but merely wrote down what struck me after reading yours" (*FL* 6:193). Fuller voiced impatience with Clarke's enthusiasm for an "all-comprehending philosophy" and fumed at the apparent elevation of "soul" over "sense" that "sich" systems assume. "'Philosophy!—If metaphysical philosophy be meant here—I do not know the Kanties but sich as Goethe and—Tieck give the senses their place, I think, ministring to and acting from the Soul and never to be lightly deemed of by her Essence-ship." Countering Clarke's reverence for "the Kanties," she praised Goethe, whose literary works were grounded in both sense and soul. Her punning use of "sich" for "such" suggests that she may know more of Kantian *Ding-an-sich* than she claimed, but the heart of her response is to resist the absolute. "'All-comprehending philosophy'? Is not that religion?—Must not all philosophy be eclectick??" (*FL* 6:192). Warning Clarke away from metaphysical systems, she took the position that philosophy is a tool for the living of life rather than an all-encompassing account of the cosmos. She embraced the idea of "philosophy" as a making of one's way, a journeying or act of building, and she reached for concrete means to characterize philosophy as a purpose-oriented form of thinking, tailored to the duties and strengths of each individual.

As she continued to respond to Clarke, it became more evident that she was looking for a code that would enable her less as a philosopher than as a doer and a friend. "I shall have faith—I do not want to *reflect* always, if reflecting must be always about one's identity, whether '*ich*' am the true ich &c." For Fuller such minute self-reflection seems a hindrance rather than a positive step in character building. It does not strengthen her, or build her confidence, or place her in a position of responsible relations with others. "I wish to arrive at that point where I can trust myself and leave off saying 'it seems to me' and boldly feel it *is* so *to me*, my character has got its natural regulator, my heart beats, my lips speak truth." This self-possession, what Emerson would later memorably explicate as "self-reliance," is not for the purposes of solitude but for the purposes of friendship. "I can walk alone," Fuller declared, "or offer my arm to a friend, or if I lean on another, it is not the debility of sickness but only wayside weariness—This is the philosophy *I* want—This much would satisfy me" (*FL* 6:193–94).

As Fuller's image of friend aiding friend suggests, she was determined to find a philosophy that would embody mutuality and relationship. As she explained to Clarke, thinking was, for her, an act of mutuality, a creative dialogue that required assertion and response. "Conversation is my natural element. I need to be called out and never think alone without imagining some companion." Although she worried that this bespoke "a second-rate mind," her self-deprecation rings false. Given her determination to insist on a philosophical practice that would allow her to "offer my arm to a friend," Fuller found strength and capability through conversation. She believed thought was always dialogue, always an experience of coming to life in response to a reciprocal call. Emerson would later recall her remarkable capacity for making conversation a genuine vehicle for philosophy. She was able to sustain, he wrote, "an absolute all-confiding intimacy between her & another, which seemed to make them both sharers of the whole horizon of each other's & of all truth" (*JMN* 11:495).

"Hard has been the part I have had to act"

Fuller's immersion in German literature with Clarke magnified two aspirations that were developing in her early twenties: the desire to be a writer and the desire to see and to know Europe. Her correspondence with Clarke played a large role in all these developments, for she found in him, and he in her, what every developing writer must have, a listening audience.

Clarke poured out his reflections on theological and philosophical issues to her without restraint, finding his way to himself through this early exercise of expression and exchange. Clarke's aspirations for the ministry were clear to both throughout the correspondence, but what of Fuller and her future? In one letter Clarke made clear his recognition of Fuller's capabilities, and most probably his sense of her budding ambitions. "I desire, Margaret, that you would edit my posthumous works and write a life of me," he jovially declared. But his high-spirited tone was also a vehicle for earnest praise. "Margaret, you are destined to be an author. I shall yet see you wholly against your will and drawn by circumstances, become the founder of an American literature! (*JFC Fuller* 35). Clarke's words "you are destined to be an author" no doubt seemed to Fuller a welcome affirmation of her growing aptitude and potential. They may also have provided confirmation, which she increasingly needed. Even as she was beginning to see the possibility of a literary career, she was coming to recognize the high price it would demand. The struggle surfaced in her reading of Goethe, whom she found a revelatory, and monumental, figure. "I am enchanted while I read," she told Clarke. Goethe "comprehends every feeling I have ever had so perfectly, expresses it so beautifully." But can the mind respond to such a totality? Where is the place of response or critique? While there is great exhilaration in such reading, there is also a certain alarm in the feeling that one has no contributory role. "When I shut the book, it seems as if I had lost my personal identity." Fuller was struggling to gain, not to lose, an identity. By contrast, "the one-sidedness, imperfection, and glow, of a mind like that of Novalis, seem refreshingly human to me." Writing seemed a path to identity, but Goethe, despite his enormous artistic and philosophical achievement, appeared at first a barrier rather than a guide.

"What can I bring?" she asked. Clarke, describing her efforts to read "the great sage." She could only resolve to "persevere in reading," in hope that "the time will come when I do not feel so overwhelmed" (*FL* 1:177).

Fuller was at this moment, as always, in search of dialogue rather than settled or authoritative truth. Novalis, then Goethe, thus became the focus of another ambition: she must come to know Europe. Her sense of a larger, more momentous world, a world in which more astute and broad-minded men and women led aware and consequential lives, came to her now principally through European authors. Fuller remembered an acquaintance from her childhood, Ellen Kilshaw from England, whose beauty and conversation were "elegant and captivating," with an active and flexible responsiveness that absorbed Fuller completely.[16] Later Fuller came to know Eliza Farrar, an influential figure in Cambridge society. Fuller's biographers, early to late, have characterized Farrar as a crucial formative influence on Fuller during a pivotal period in her life.[17] Farrar was, as Thomas Wentworth Higginson wrote, "a woman of uncommon character and cultivation, who had lived much in Europe, and who, with no children of her own, did many good services for the children of her friends."[18] Farrar recognized in Fuller a young woman whose intellectual brilliance was marred by gracelessness and a lack of self-restraint; she vowed to remake her. "Something in Margaret's earnest awkwardness and sincerity," Joan von Mehren explains, moved Farrar to take her "permanently in charge."[19] Fuller found in Farrar not only a kind and supportive friend but also closer access to a cultured and artistic world that she desired. Farrar's intellectual attainments, cosmopolitan sophistication, and firm self-confidence were important models for Fuller. She was also a woman with a genius for sociability, and among her greatest gifts to Fuller were her introductions. Three of these would have a powerful impact on Fuller's development: Farrar's niece Anna Barker, her young friend Samuel Gray Ward, and a minister and lecturer of rising prominence, Ralph Waldo Emerson.

Given Fuller's emerging ambitions as a writer, it was also significant that Farrar was a successful author. She was best known for an influential book of manners, *The Young Lady's Friend* (1836), a guidebook to household management, social etiquette, and personal development.

While a modern reader is likely to become engrossed, for better or worse, in the aspects of nineteenth-century upper-class housekeeping detailed by Farrar, her real goal, announced prominently in the book's opening pages, was of particular importance to Fuller. "The great business of early education is to form habits of industry, to train the mind to find pleasure in intellectual effort, and to inspire a love of knowledge for its own sake."[20] Farrar regarded manners and social forms, modes of experience that her culture regarded as part of the feminine sphere, as in fact dangerous obstacles to women's self-development. That development must, she insisted, be primarily intellectual, and *The Young Lady's Friend* championed both wide-ranging education and ongoing intellectual cultivation for women. She cautioned her readers not to leave school at an early age and regarded continuing self-education as imperative for women. Farrar's attraction to the intellectually gifted and earnestly striving young Fuller is easy to understand. Farrar's emphasis on women's education and mental culture reinforced Fuller's own Unitarian ethos of self-culture, and it would become one of the key principles in her later demand for the liberation for women.

Farrar became an important lifeline to Cambridge for Fuller when her father made the fateful decision to move his family from Cambridge to a farm near Groton in 1833. This was a dramatic change of course for Timothy Fuller, who had been a successful attorney, served in the Massachusetts Senate (1813–1817), and the US House of Representatives (1817–1825), and had run, unsuccessfully, for lieutenant governor of Massachusetts in 1832.[21] While his election defeat may have been the immediate catalyst for the move, it was one he had long considered, as Fuller's biographer Charles Capper notes (Capper 1:119). He saw it in part as a scholarly retreat in which he could devote his energies to writing a Jeffersonian history of the United States, while also enacting the Jeffersonian dream of self-sufficient independence on the land. Margaret resented the move bitterly and began to recognize, with alarm, that the fragile learned life that she had constructed in Cambridge was now threatened by rural exile. Plunged into a double drudgery of serving as tutor-governess to four younger siblings and as family seamstress, she had to use every measure of her self-discipline to maintain her intellectual life, her drive for self-development, and the network of friendships in Cambridge that were vital to her. The depth of her distress in Groton is clear from many comments in her letters to Clarke, who had himself left for a pastorate in Louisville. She unreservedly poured out her disappointment, abandoning her positive attitude for an agonized confession of her misery. "And you are gone—and you will prosper—you will improve daily," she wrote. "It is well—just what I wished and yet I regret your departure surprisingly. I am not just where I have so often wished to be—I am alone" (*FL* 6:209). She missed Clarke personally, of course, but her "I am alone" should not be taken as the cry of a jilted lover. Fuller was a woman stranded from meaningful interaction, denied the conversation that was sustenance for her. The lack of real conversation threatened the path of development that she had undertaken. Learning was, she felt, a dialogic process, and without dialogue, her receptivity as a thinker and her capacity to grow through self-expression would be inhibited. Deprived of the key to self-expression, a like-minded and sympathetic conversant, Fuller felt herself "being used up by ounces" in Groton. "I am dejected and uneasy when I see no results from my daily existence but I am suffocated and lost when I have not the bright feeling of progression" (*FL* 6:216). Reading Goethe and recognizing that he lived, as she put it, "always with some engrossing object of pursuit" (*FL* 6:216), she was instead beginning to feel the waste of her promise. Her youthful capacity to grow had been "suffocated" before its time. Lamenting her despair in terms of a broken process of self-development, she saw the dreams of intellectual and literary achievement, implanted in her from early childhood, slipping away. "O pray for me," she implored Clarke. "Hard has been the part I have had to act, far more so than you ever knew" (*FL* 6:221).

Fuller's isolation and resultant crisis in Groton had been almost wholly the creation of her father, who was also the source of her high intellectual aspirations, and the provider of the early tutelage that had given her the linguistic training that was the grounding for literary success. Despite her building resentment of him, she had dutifully served, and largely succeeded, as tutor to her younger siblings at Groton, and she continued to have a special relationship with him. Forceful personalities, both of them, with willful determination and an inclination for command, they seemed to be heading toward an inevitable collision as life in Groton continued. But fate was moving more quickly.

In the fall of 1835, Margaret Fuller was stricken with typhoid fever and brought near death, a crisis grave enough to move her father to tell her, "You have defects, as all mortals have, but I do not know that you have a single fault" (Capper 1:158). However measured this praise, it was extraordinary, given its source. Three days after Margaret's recovery, Timothy Fuller himself died quite suddenly from cholera. The sudden loss of her father was a profound emotional blow and would be a lifelong source of distress. She and her family would soon come to realize that he had left them with very little money. Her apparently growing resentment of him thus had to be repressed, in both her grief for him and her recognition that she would have to act as the key support, emotionally and financially, of her siblings and her mother. One incident, novelistic in its power, captures both the intensity and the complexity of Fuller's reaction to her father's unexpected death. Fuller's mother, Higginson recorded, "used to tell the story, to the end of her days," of how Fuller brought "the younger children together around the lifeless form of her father, and, kneeling, pledged herself to God that if she had ever been ungrateful or unfilial to her father, she would atone for it by fidelity to her brothers and sisters. This vow," Higginson commented, "she surely kept" (Higginson 54). As her biographers tell us, she became the head of her family. Fuller was haunted by a sense of ungratefulness. She had, in a deeply ironic twist, become her father, assuming his role while being forced to relinquish her own goals and desires. As Paula Blanchard perceptively observes, "guilt fueled the spirit of renunciation" with which Fuller undertook those duties.[22] She was torn between mourning for her father and guilt-tinged resentment for his sudden abandonment of her. But she took on her new role with courage and determination, qualities that would define the course of her life and thought.

"The law of life in that land was beauty"

In May of 1841, some six years after her father's death, Fuller wrote her "Autobiographical Romance," an assessment of years of turmoil, grieving, self-disapproval, and self-examination. Paternal authority was its underlying root.[23] The "Autobiographical Romance" was not published until after Fuller's death, as the opening text of the biography that Clarke, Emerson, and William Henry Channing hoped would be a monument to Fuller's life and achievement. In this work Fuller was opening an examination of the individuality of one woman but also an exploration of the life of women and their circumstances. As Sidonie Smith has explained, the self that women had to take up in the process of self-writing had been conceived principally as male throughout history. To articulate her experience, a female author had to interrogate, explicitly or implicitly, this culturally inscribed maleness of the narrated self. The self-revelatory writing of nineteenth-century women was thus an implicit "poetics of resistance," Smith maintains, in which writers acted as both "creative sign makers" and "agents of contestation."[24] Fuller's autobiography seems a remarkably self-aware example of this dynamic, particularly in its analysis of self-development as a struggle against paternal authority.

The words "My Father" open the "Autobiographical Romance," as a recognition of Timothy Fuller's central role in the early shaping of his daughter's identity and an acknowledgment that she had to measure herself against her father and his expectations to come to a complete self-understanding. Fuller's portrait of him is a stinging rebuke, but it also carries a certain respect and sympathy. Reading the letters that a very young Fuller wrote to her father, Megan Marshall found an "anxious, eager-to-please seven-year-old" child, hoping to placate her father after his long day. His advice was to excel in all her efforts, and she followed this guidance in so far as it was associated with writing. It was a deep but difficult relationship.[25] Most importantly, Fuller was coming to understand her father as a man whose character and experience revealed cultural barriers and limitations that he was unable, or unwilling, to overcome. Her struggle with him, therefore, was also a struggle against deeply rooted cultural values and expectations and an embedded hierarchy of social power. Timothy Fuller was, she wrote, "a lawyer and a politician" who was "largely endowed with that sagacious energy" typical of New England culture. His own father, a clergyman, had firmly believed "the great object of his ambition was to send his sons to college," and that passion for formal and institutionalized education was clearly imbued in Timothy, who hoped to make his first child "the heir of all he knew" (*EMF* 24, 26). This ambition was grounded, Fuller contended, not only in her father's character but also in the society that formed it. "As a Lawyer, again, the ends constantly presented were to work for distinction in the community, and for the means of supporting a family. To be an honored citizen, and to have a home on earth, were made the great aims of existence." Fuller's carefully crafted language should be noted. Her father's "ends" were "presented" to him; some external force "made" or constructed his "aims of existence" (*EMF* 24). Fuller's larger purpose was to make her father a representative figure, a man who embodied culturally accepted values and practices that were much more powerful than those of any individual.

Her capacity to see her father in this light was an important intellectual breakthrough; it meant that she understood that her battle for self-possession was not with a particular man but with a social structure and its ingrained assumptions about the nature and differing roles of women and men. Those assumptions had, she believed, rendered her father a man of duty and social place without access to "the deeper fountains of the soul." He was a man of surface but not depth, of "outward relations" but without an interpersonal or spiritual dimension. "In the more delicate and individual relations, he never approached but two mortals, my mother and myself" (*EMF* 24). This inner poverty, which Fuller came to see as a signpost for American culture, was alarming. She identified his "one great mistake" of attempting to bring "forward the intellect as early as possible." Pushed to the limit of her capacity and denied necessary rest because of her father's lengthy workdays, Fuller suffered, she believed, "a premature development of the brain, that made me a 'youthful prodigy' by day, and by night a victim of spectral illusions, nightmare, and somnambulism." Shifting from the first-person perspective with which she had constructed the foregoing narrative, Fuller began to describe the fate of "this child," misunderstood by parents and other relatives and driven into a state of extreme stress and agitation (*EMF* 26, 27). Fuller's shift of narrative perspective is notable and somewhat puzzling. It may reflect her personal reluctance to deal directly with her terrifying nightmares, and it may also signal her intention to make herself a representative figure, the "child" who corresponds to the "father" of the narrative. Her description of her psychic trauma borrows from the gothic, making the mind and its dreams a chamber of horrors. "The child" was forced to bed, to confront "colossal faces advancing slowly towards her, the eyes dilating, and each feature swelling loathsomely as they came." She described "horses trampling over her" and "trees that dripped with blood" (an image she ascribed to her reading of Virgil). "No wonder," she commented, "the child arose and walked in her sleep, moaning all over the house" (*EMF* 27). Ghost-like, the injured "child" haunted the broken household, signifying the loss of her own well-being and of the family's domestic harmony.

While transcendentalism is associated with a sunny optimism, a body of writing in which images of dawn, awakening, light, and transparency set the tone, Fuller's nightmarish images are the kind of dark romanticism that one might expect of contemporaries such as Poe and Hawthorne. In her darker version of transcendentalism, the aspiration toward self-culture and perpetual spiritual expansion sours into hallucinatory horror and intense suffering. It suggests extreme stress rather than fulfillment. Fuller was familiar with the key visual image of transcendentalism, Emerson's "transparent eye-ball" in *Nature*, which embodied seeing, lucidity, and an empowered transcendence of material barriers.[26] The "child" that Fuller described had been rendered insecure and vulnerable. Her natural path of development was distorted. The "colossal faces" with "eyes dilating" that she described seem to be a deliberate reversal of Emerson's depiction of transcendent elation and vision. Her account of her dreams is notably material and corporeal—faces, eyes, and pools of blood that "plashed over her feet" and expanded until "she dreamed it would reach her lips" (*EMF* 27). Rather than dissolving rapturously into benign countryside, as Emerson imagined, Fuller slowly drowned in a rising pool of blood. The weirdest of these nightmares were the "often" repeated images of a funeral in which "the child's" mother took the place of her dead sister in burial: "Often she dreamed of following to the grave the body of her mother, as she had done with that of her sister, and woke to find the pillow drenched in tears" (*EMF* 27).

Where does one begin with this entanglement of identities and deaths? The dream visits her grief, but it is also an expression of fear for the loss of her mother. In its motif of a return to the graveside, the dream also suggests Fuller's concern with her own mortality, the continuing sense of insecurity that her baby sister's death had brought. It is of course significant that all three of the figures connected with death—the child, her mother, and her sister—are female. The dream seems to suggest her fear of a world made utterly masculine by her father's powerful will. This aspect of the dream echoes Fuller's unrest with her conversion into her father's surrogate son. As we read the nightmare, we recognize that Fuller's deep apprehension about her identity emphasized the question of gender as a crucial but unarticulated concept in her account of herself.

In the "Autobiographical Romance," Fuller had come to recognize that her father's intervention in her early development had deprived her of a "natural childhood" (*EMF* 27) and set her on an unbalanced course of future development. His rigorous methods, she wrote, "had prevented the harmonious development of my bodily powers, and checked my growth," thus causing her "continual headache, weakness and nervous affections, of all kinds" (*EMF* 26). Fuller had come to realize that her father had thwarted this process with his demanding mentoring and unrelenting expectations. His intention had been to discipline and train his daughter's mind, but he had in fact injured her body in doing so. Fuller identified her wounds not only as "nervous affections" but as physical or corporeal ailments as well. Her "masculine" accomplishments as a scholar and master of languages and texts thus came, she reasoned, at the price of her physical health and fortitude. Fuller had eventually recognized that this kind of learning had been alien to her in important ways. "He had no conception of the subtle and indirect motions of imagination and feeling" and thus pushed against "the natural unfolding of my character, which was fervent, of strong grasp, and disposed to infatuation and self-forgetfulness" (*EMF* 28). She had been chained to a utilitarian world, but one without imagination.

This world was, however, founded on books, and through them Fuller discovered ways to nourish an inner life. In Greek mythology, she caught glimpses of a world in which "the law of life in that land was beauty" (*EMF* 30, 31), and in Shakespeare she found even more sustenance for her imagination.[27] Her reading of *Romeo and Juliet* at age eight epitomized her hunger for the imaginative and the aesthetic and her determination to take her own path despite her father's strictures. Finding her rapt in a book on a Sunday afternoon and realizing that she was reading Shakespeare, her father rebuked her, declaring, "That's no book for a Sunday; go put it away and take another." Fuller complied, briefly, but, she recalled, as the Shakespearean characters and dialogue "burnt in my brain," she returned to the banned volume. Her defiance resulted in an early dismissal to bed, but there she continued to remember "the free flow of life, sudden and graceful dialogue, and forms, whether grotesque or fair, seen in the broad luster of [Shakespeare's] imagination." The play ignited her, and she saw in it, as she would later see in the work of many other authors, that writing was "the life I seemed born to live" (*EMF* 34).

Fuller's description of her childhood battle with her father has been given great historical attention, but a quite different picture of family life emerges when she speaks of her mother. "The happiest haunt of my childish years," she remembered, was her mother's garden. This small enclosure was a tender and nourishing place, "my mother's delight" (*EMF* 31). Fuller's interjection of this female alternative to her father's masculine world signaled her awareness of gender as a shaping force for women. "Here I felt at home," she wrote, expressing a sense of belonging and peace utterly absent from her accounts of her dealings with her father. In the garden, she recalled, "my thoughts could lie callow in the nest, and only be fed and kept warm, not called to fly or sing before the time" (*EMF* 32). The garden's flowers represented the evocative aspects of women's culture, and she "loved to gaze on the roses, the violets, the lilies, the pinks; my mother's hand had planted them, and they bloomed for me" (*EMF* 32).

Fuller's embrace of the flowers suggests not only her love of nature and beauty but also the sense of loneliness that pervades the narrative of her childhood, which she called a "bookish and solitary life" (*EMF* 37). That loneliness is emphasized indirectly in her discussion of three friends, Shakespeare, Cervantes, and Molière, "great minds" who "came to me in kindness," to guarantee that "my youth was not unfriended" (*EMF* 36). Yet such friends, as she seems to suggest, only underline her fundamental aloneness. Hers was not a loneliness of isolation, since she was the oldest daughter in a growing family whose lives were by no means lived in seclusion. But as she confessed in retrospect, "I do wish that I had read no books at all till later,—that I had lived with toys, and played in the open air." Books robbed her, she felt, of experience, even though she had sought life in them. "With me, much of life was devoured in the bud" (*EMF* 37). Given the extraordinary life she would live, this dispirited statement now seems far amiss.

The "Autobiographical Romance" ends with Fuller's impassioned description of Ellen Kilshaw, who had provided her first glimpse of beauty, grace, and artistic ability. Woven into Fuller's praise of Kilshaw is her recognition of this meeting as an important early awakening. She reconstructed, through her memory of Kilshaw, her recognition of encounter, conversation, and relation as the keys to self-knowledge and self-fulfillment, the fundamental goals of philosophy itself. "The first sight, the first knowledge of such a person was intoxication" (*EMF* 38), she wrote. She could now release herself fully in admiration and devotion. "My thoughts were fixed on her with all the force of my nature. It was my first real interest in my kind, and it engrossed me wholly" (*EMF* 38). One revealing incident suggests Fuller's use of her memory of Kilshaw in the self-construction that the "Autobiographical Romance" represented. "One time I had been passing the afternoon with her," Fuller recalled. "She had been playing to me on the harp, and I sat listening in happiness almost unbearable." Left alone when Kilshaw was called away to greet some visitors, she began to look at the book Kilshaw had been reading earlier that afternoon, Sir Walter Scott's *Guy Mannering*. She read "with the feeling of continuing our mutual existence by passing my eyes over the same page where hers had been." Her claiming of Kilshaw's book is a claiming of Kilshaw herself, a merging of their separate eyes and identities. But the passage Kilshaw had been reading, ominously, was the description of the plight of a child lost on a rugged seacoast. "I was the little Harry Bartram," Fuller remembered, "and had lost her,—all I had to lose,—and sought her vainly in long dark caves that had no end, plashing through the water" (*EMF* 39). The "Autobiographical Romance" ends abruptly with this overwrought account of friendship found and friendship lost. This was, as we will see, uppermost in Fuller's mind in 1840, when she had brought together a circle of friends into an emotionally complex and powerful series of interpersonal bondings and betrayals. We might surmise that Fuller's entire effort in the "Autobiographical Romance" was to write her way into a place in which the power of friendship and the pain of loss could be expressed. "I can tell little else of this time,—indeed I remember little," Fuller wrote, "except the state of feeling in which I lived. For I lived, and when this is the case, there is little to tell in the form of thought" (*EMF* 40). Her memory of Kilshaw no doubt presaged "the state of feeling" in which she lived in 1840, and would feel again in Europe, when she finally arrived in the later 1840s. As she explored the resonant memory of this deeply significant experience, she linked it to a larger theory of the life-building capacity of deep human interaction, the first necessity, she believed, of the awakened and spiritually vital life. We meet "a succession of persons through our lives, all of whom have some peculiar errand to us," she observed. While we must be aware of and attentive to the "outer circle" of these acquaintances, "with whom we stand in no real relation," our lives are defined by "a nearer group," whose character shapes us. These friends, "beings born under the same star, and bound with us in a common destiny," are, Fuller had come to believe, a part of us and we of them. This vision radically redefines human experience in interpersonal and communal, rather than individual, terms. "There is no separation," Fuller declared. "The same thought is given at the same moment to both,—indeed, it is born of the meeting, and would not otherwise have been called into existence at all!" (*EMF* 40). These relationships are self-making, generating from relationship new forms of consciousness and discernment. Such friends "not only know themselves more, but *are* more for having met, and regions of their being, which would else have laid sealed in cold obstruction, burst into leaf and bloom and song" (*EMF* 40–41).

CHAPTER 2
The "Flame-like" Soul

The Law of Creative Activity

Although it was a moving depiction of her traumatic childhood, the "Autobiographical Romance" tells us more about Fuller at age thirty, when it was written. It is a document of grief and of healing, suggesting her struggle for self-awareness and purpose in Groton and its dramatic intensification after her father's death. In the aftermath of that shock, she found herself head of the Fuller household, with worries over inadequate monetary resources. This financial crisis, complicating her grief with further resentment, impinged severely on her vocational ambitions. Despite her suffering, she nevertheless made remarkable growth and achievement, securing her place as an author, a lecturer, and a rising public figure in New England's nascent women's movement.

Fuller found her principal guide in Goethe, whose message of ever-renewing creativity and growth amplified the code of self-culture that was her religious underpinning. Her aims were high, and she measured herself in terms of the intellectual aspirations instilled by her father and reinforced, when possible, by her interaction with ambitious and scholarly men like Clarke and Hedge. But the institutional support open to them through Harvard and the New England ministry was unavailable to her. Pushed back on her own capabilities and will, she forged a way forward through her study of German and her deepening interest in Goethe. The studies she had begun enthusiastically with Clarke in Cambridge became crucial to her after the move to Groton in 1833. Charles Capper mentions that her reading was, as Emerson admiringly noted, "at a rate like Gibbon's" (Capper 1:127).

Despite her appreciation of Groton's pastoral beauty and her devotion to her family, her letters from the early 1830s show a suffocating loneliness and resentment of her isolation. This entrapment fed her hunger for Goethe, a writer who embodied both an Olympian freedom of thought and a cosmopolitan engagement with human character. Writing Clarke from her Groton imprisonment in 1833, she expressed "an earnest desire to live as [Goethe] did—always to have some engrossing object of pursuit—I do sympathize deeply with a mind in that state." She felt, in contrast, "used up by ounces" and "suffocated and lost," devoid of the "bright feeling of progression" that she sensed in Goethe (*FL* 6:216). This suffocation reflected her deep conviction that true "freedom" always lay in the possibility of new and deeper relationships, which was not a possibility in her present isolation. "Verily there is no escaping from the dust and weariness and burden of this state of seclusion—Free?—Vain thought!" (*FL* 6:215).

She believed that Goethe had found ways to pursue experience that had so far eluded or been denied her. "How often I have thought if I could see Goethe and tell him my state of mind he would support and guide me—he would be able to understand" (*FL* 6:212). He was a kindred soul, and reading him confirmed her alarm that she had lost her direction to the deeper life that was in her nature. "It seems to me as if the mind of Goethe had embraced the universe," she declared to Clarke in an August 1832 letter. "I have felt this lately, on reading his lyric poems. I am enchanted while I read. He comprehends every feeling I have ever had so perfectly, expresses it so beautifully; but when I shut the book, it seems as if I had lost my personal identity; all my feelings linked with such an immense variety that belong to beings I had thought so different" (*FL* 1:177). As her knowledge of Goethe grew, she retained some reservations, as she explained in an 1834 letter, probably to Clarke. "I do not know our Goethe yet. I have changed my opinion about his religious views many times. Sometimes I am tempted to think that it is only his wonderful knowledge of human nature which has excited in me such reverence for his philosophy" (*FL* 1:198). Her independence of mind was, of course, very Goethean in its refusal to systematize or codify ideas at the cost of renewing greater vitality.

By the time she moved to Groton, Fuller believed that she had mastered German well enough to translate him. This was, as we can now understand, a decisive moment, because her translations established her as a figure of authority. The first of her translations was of *Tasso*, Goethe's dramatization of the arrest and confinement of the sixteenth-century Italian poet Torquato Tasso, whose impulsive and reckless behavior cost him his place in the ducal court of Ferrara. Fuller completed the translation during her first summer at Groton in 1833, and it circulated in manuscript among the transcendentalists throughout the middle 1830s. To a group hungry for material on German literature and philosophy, the translation was both informative and deeply impressive, establishing Fuller's facility in German literature and setting the terms for the early phase of her friendship with Emerson. Christina Zwarg was the first critic to recognize Fuller's translations as acts of "social intervention," a literary intercession that demonstrated a new pathway for social and political development.[1] Zwarg's reading of "the complex series of impulses that went into her decision to translate this particular drama" explains how Fuller used the text to investigate questions of gender and literary recognition that were of growing importance to her.[2] Among the questions that Goethe's drama pursues is the place of the poet, and of literature, in society, a question of importance to Clarke, Emerson, Hedge and other young men whose incipient careers blended religion with aspects of literary culture. "Tasso" became, Zwarg observed, a name that marked "the Concord circle" of literary aspirants, capturing in it "the signal of their own complicated interaction" (Zwarg 69).

The character Tasso, a poet and an outcast as Goethe presented him, also seemed to embody Fuller's own anguish at her repeated failure to attain what she deemed sufficient understanding from others. This pain would deepen over the next decade. In 1842 she reviewed a biography of Tasso for *The Dial* and included in that review excerpts of her still unpublished translation. Her characterization of Tasso, grounded in Goethe's realization of him as a romantic misfit, suggested much about her own self-appraisal. "There are other natures that must always act and feel before they can know," she wrote of the incendiary Tasso. "Flame-like the soul shoots up from amid such fuel as existence offers; it sinks as suddenly as it rose; it kindles afresh in its dull bed, and bursts forth more vehement than ever; it retires into reflection only when all is burned that was there to be burned; glimmering more calmly amid the ashes." It seems that Goethe's version of Tasso served Fuller as a mirror to her own ungovernable passions. More tellingly, she saw the poet, like herself, paying the price of abandonment because of that fiery nature. A disposition like Tasso's could be "loved with constancy only by a nature large enough to understand, larger if not so deep as his own," she wrote, adding this dark surmise: "Whether he found such an one is doubtful."[3] These words explain Fuller's attraction to Goethe's antihero in the 1830s as she faced isolation in Groton.

The recognition that Fuller gained from the *Tasso* translation no doubt reinforced her ambition to write what would have been the first biography of Goethe in English. In 1835, still in communication with Clarke, she coyly urged him to take on that very task. "Why don't you write a *Life* of Goethe in two vols octo accompanied by criticisms on his works." Even though "this vision swims often before mine own eyes," she deferred, with calculated modesty, to Clarke's greater "eloquence" (*FL* 6:260). He responded as she no doubt hoped by encouraging her to write one herself.[4] Fuller believed that a European trip was essential for her to locate the required information for a complete biography, and she nurtured hopes for a trip to Europe. Those hopes were pinned on the generosity of Eliza Farrar, who was formulating plans for a journey that already included two younger friends, Anna Barker and Samuel Gray Ward, who would have an immense impact on Fuller in the coming years.[5] Still feeling stifled in Groton, Fuller had set her heart on this journey, which was closely intertwined with her literary ambitions and her sense of personal development. But the sudden death of her father on October 1, 1835, shattered her plans for the European trip. His loss did not immediately crush Fuller's dream, but it died slowly, and with anguish, over the winter of 1835–36 as the realities of her family's precarious financial situation became clear. Still hopeful in February 1836, Fuller told Clarke: "I am shocked to perceive that you think I am *writing* a life of Goethe. No, indeed!" She needed further information on Goethe's first years in Weimar, and access to "the books that have been written about him in Germany, by friend or foe." Fuller continues, "I thought I must get some idea of the history of philosophical opinion in Germany, that I might be able to judge of the influence it exercised upon his mind" (*FL* 1:244–45).

Only two months later, though, Fuller had begun to face the bitter reality that she could not afford the trip.[6] "How can I get the information I want unless I go to Europe?" she wrote Clarke, in a tone that nears desperation. Information "about his life" would be hard to get in provincial America, she feared, especially since information on Goethe inevitably led to questions about his love affairs and his marriage, forbidden territory for discussion between the sexes in New England. "*Gentlemen* and *ladies* usually talk a good deal but apart from one another," she told Clarke, using the opportunity to plead with him for frankness. "I am very destitute of what is commonly called modesty" (*FL* 6:287). After much agonizing, she abandoned her hopes for the journey in May of 1836, explaining, "Circumstances have decided that I must not go to Europe, and shut upon me the door, as I think, forever, to the scenes I could have loved" (*FL* 6:287). These circumstances not only barred her from Europe but also seemed to threaten her creative life itself. "What I can do with my pen, I know not. At present I feel no confidence or hope. The expectations so many have been led to cherish by my conversational powers, I am disposed to deem ill-founded. I do not think I can produce a valuable work" (*FL* 1:254).

One remarkable document from this period, a letter, or a letter draft, or perhaps a prayerlike memorandum to herself, signaled the determination that Fuller began to summon as she reoriented herself and refused to abandon her Germanic studies.[7] Written after Eliza Farrar and her husband, John, had departed on the voyage she had so fervently wished to take, she pledged to see few people and to concentrate fully on her work. Fuller consigned her earlier plans to a youth now lost. "All hopes of traveling I have dismissed—All youthful hopes of every kind I have pushed away from my thoughts—I will not, if I can help it, lose an hour in castle-building and repining—Too much of that already!" Separating the allure of travel from the business of scholarship, she reconsecrated herself to German literature, renewing the pledge that she had taken earlier to learn the language. "I have now a pursuit of immediate importance to the German language and literature I will give my undivided attention." Shaken profoundly when Europe vanished, she now renewed her vows. That Fuller undertook this study with profound seriousness is clear. But her prayerful appeal for steadiness and focus also suggests her continuing emotional turmoil. "Please God to keep my mind composed," she begged. "Oh! Keep me steady in an honorable ambition" (*FL* 1:241).

It seems as if Fuller's prayer was quickly answered. In his edition of Fuller's letters, Robert N. Hudspeth assigns a probable date of 1836 to this manuscript. Fuller's first substantial critical essay on German literature was published in July of 1836, an important token of her renewing sense of purpose.[8] Her "Present State of German Literature" was a breakthrough essay that should now be recognized among Perry Miller's "Annus Mirabilis" compositions, those 1836 writings that generated the transcendentalist movement.[9] Fuller's literary contribution to the evolving transcendentalist conversation brought a new vitality to the exchange of ideas by bringing modern literature, as well as modern theology, into focus. Her essay appeared in *American Monthly Magazine* in July, the month when she met Emerson. She spent three weeks with the Emerson family, and it was there that Fuller first heard parts of Emerson's nearly completed manuscript of *Nature*. This meeting began her deep and sometimes tumultuous friendship with Emerson, one of the most significant literary friendships of the era.[10] Emerson knew of her *Tasso* translation and her command of German literature from Clarke and Hedge, and they shared social connections with Eliza Farrar and Elizabeth Palmer Peabody. Fuller had followed Emerson's career as a minister and lecturer with interest. She was drawn to him in part because of his dramatic resignation of his Boston pulpit in 1832, an act that bespoke a kind of rebellious integrity.[11] She was also aware of his reputation as an eloquent and affecting preacher and lecturer. It seems fitting that she met him when he was nearing the completion of *Nature*. It was a book in which he would weave the sermon, the poem, the philosophical treatise, the oration, and elements of autobiographical narrative and dramatic dialogue into a manifesto of the new philosophy. These poetic dimensions of Emerson's writings—his ability to register the widest range of emotions, from elation to despair, and to call up the mysterious and the elusive—set him apart from his transcendentalist contemporaries. Like Clarke, Hedge, and other restless Unitarian ministers whom Fuller knew, Emerson was pushing the boundaries of theological speculation. For Fuller, only Emerson's explorations seemed infused with the imaginative energy that had drawn her to Goethe and Novalis.

This thirst for new vision and absorbing expression permeated Fuller's essay. "We rejoice to see among us symptoms of a growing interest in German literature," she wrote, describing this awakening as a "counterpoise" to the "so-called prosperity" that was turning "the American mind into a spiritual spinning jenny, set in motion by no higher impulse than that of utility, understood in its lowest sense—a vulgar, sordid, eating, and drinking utility" (MF Pres 2). Americans might not appear to be suffering, but their superficial cheer was an inadequate answer to existence. "The United States of America are happy, or, as it is pithily said, flourishing; but there are other realms still more happy and flourishing in amaranthine bloom; we mean the realms of intellectual life" (MF Pres 3). Intellectual complacency and spiritual vacuity, by-products of narrow American utilitarianism, were putting Americans at risk of "learning to consider our minds as no more than parts of one great machine." As a consequence, the nation's citizens were in danger "of losing independence of opinion and action," a sinister and largely self-imposed collective enslavement. Fuller argued that the cause of this malaise was a neglect of the inner life, which could flourish only through cultivation and constant renewal. "We are not merely springs and wheels, which, when put in certain places and kept oiled, will undoubtedly and undoubtingly do their work and fulfil their destination. No! In each one of us there is a separate principle of vitality, which must be fostered" (MF Pres 3).

Goethe's fiery counter to this numbing utilitarianism made him, Fuller declared, "*the* great original mind of the age" (MF Pres 11). That he challenged convention, even sacrosanct moral codes, was essential to his achievement, she argued. What disturbed Goethe's zealous moral censors was his determination to pursue his art without preaching and didacticism. He presented both character and event in a way that demanded that his readers measure his innovations against their own recognition of human experience, not against an abstract code. Goethe's critics accused him of "wanting a moral sense because he paints vice as well as virtue exactly as it exists without bringing himself on the stage, either by pious horror or interesting enthusiasm" (MF Pres 10). As she immersed herself more deeply in his work, she grew in her conviction of his cosmopolitan openness, his artistic honesty, and his capacity to authenticate human aspiration.

"Fresh creative life"

Three years would pass before Fuller published her next significant work on German literature, a translation of Johann Peter Eckermann's *Conversations with Goethe*.[12] This was a portrayal of a sage-like Goethe offering conversational guidance on art and life. Fuller recognized the importance of the vocal form of Eckermann's book. For her, the printed word derived its power from its roots in spoken exchange. She had found other adherents of the philosophy of conversation in Bronson Alcott's innovative teaching at his Temple School and in the group forming around Emerson, Hedge, and George Ripley. Eckermann's depiction of Goethe in dialogue furthered her conviction that sincere conversation was the most powerful form of intellectual expression.

Fuller began the Eckermann translation as a strategic move in the cultural war enveloping Goethe, a conflict ever more deeply intertwined with her own identity and ambition. Goethe's reputation was under ferocious assault by the New England clergy, led by Andrews Norton, the prominent Harvard biblical scholar who would later turn his censure on Emerson to provoke what became the Transcendental Controversy. Norton's attack was a prelude to the later strike on Emerson's "Divinity School Address," which Norton saw as "the strange state of things existing about us in the literary and religious world."[13] He feared that Goethe's growing fame in Germany might generate a conversion to his moral sentiments in America, and he leveled an attack on transcendentalism before the movement quite knew itself as such.

Goethe could have had no more valiant and perceptive champion than Fuller, but her advocacy was, even so, a troubled one. The attacks of Norton and others raised questions not only about the moral nature of his writings but about his personal conduct as well. Fuller had heard only scattered hints and rumors about his long premarital relationship with his eventual wife, Christiane Vulpius, and could get very little frank discussion about it from her male friends. Given her impatience with America's provincialism, Goethe's cosmopolitan freedom was part of his appeal, and his fictional characters seemed to her both genuine and moving. But her admiration was flickering, and at times she sensed the risk of blindly endorsing a man who lived by a code she could not accept.

Fuller's preface to *Conversations with Goethe* stands as one of her most underappreciated essays. Expanding on her "Present State of German Literature," Fuller declared Goethe the priest of a creed of creative endeavor and ethical duty. With the condemnations of Norton in mind, she identified the source of Goethe's literary power as "the feeling of fresh creative life at work there" (*MFE* xi). The presentation of a Goethe of intellectual independence and generative energy provided her with an incisive response to the religiously grounded suspicions of him. He was, she stipulated, not indifferent in his religion, but he refused to subordinate "the intellectual to the spiritual." He was instead an intellect in constant search, a thinker who "always sought for unity" between spirit and mind but never rested philosophically. "A creative activity was his law," she explained, setting out a credo that had become her own as well. While attuned to the "spiritual beauty in the human character," Goethe understood human weakness and folly, and refused to represent life "with partiality." His portrayal of men and women did not sacrifice complex truth for an idealized spirituality. Fuller, who disdained art in which human experience was censored, relished this frankness. "His God was rather the creative and upholding than the paternal spirit; his religion, that all his powers must be unfolded" (*MFE* xiii). This had become her God as well. She shared the refusal of a paternal God with her transcendentalist colleagues, who were actively searching for new religious language to replace those exhausted by Christianity.

Embracing a transitive, metamorphic God, known through energy and creative power rather than person or being, Fuller entered ground that, as Emerson had discovered, was explosively sensitive. In her Eckermann essay she conceded that Goethe was "not a Christian" in the narrowest sense because he consistently refused to affirm dogma that was contrary to reason. But she identified him with one foundational belief that, she felt, saved him from the condition of skepticism and pure relativism. "In the most trying occasions of his life, Goethe referred to 'the great Idea of Duty which alone can hold us upright'" (*MFE* xiii). This kind of consecrated work, rooted in relation with others and a responsibility to them, was Fuller's aspiration. She also found the quality of self-sacrifice to be a larger duty in Goethe's *Elective Affinities*, a novel that was of profound importance to her. She recognized great redemptive power in "the virgin Ottilia, who immolates herself to avoid the possibility of spotting her thoughts with passion" (*MFE* xiv). Ottilie's self-control was not just an effort to maintain her own purity but an acceptance of her sense of responsibility for the well-being of others.

While Goethe was a champion of "duty," he was by no means a defender of unexamined codes of conduct. This was, for Fuller, a crucial distinction. In full rebellion against maudlin, formulaic writing, in which New England was drowning in the 1830s, she asked instead for a literature of engagement and interaction, which elevated reading to a high, exacting discipline. Literature could be a powerful tool for moral culture, not because it provided answers but because it placed the reader at the point of choosing, and thus awakened the ethical imagination. "Goethe was not what is called a spiritual writer" (*MFE* xiv), she argued, meaning that his work was not reductively dogmatic but open to and aware of the turbulence of experience. He was not in denial of the flesh or at war with it. He was in this sense a kind of anti-Puritan, whose power and appeal resided in a sympathetic realism about human experience. This clear and nonjudgmental vision was, Fuller argued, the quality that had attracted much hostile criticism. "Those who cannot draw their moral for themselves had best leave his books alone," she cautioned. "They require the power as life does" (*MFE* xiv). Fuller's ironic warning typified the cutting wit that her contemporaries noted in her conversation. She turned Goethe's critics into mental weaklings, unable to discern moral truth unless it was gift wrapped for them. She detected an underlying cowardice, a fear that their comfortable traditions and codes could not withstand objective inquiry and the test of experience. Fuller thus showed Goethe's worldliness as both a philosophy and a standard of artistic creation. "This advantage only does he give, or intend to give you," she wrote, "of looking at life brought into a compass convenient to your eye, by a great observer and artist." Life is available only to readers prepared and willing to see it, at those moments "uninterrupted by action, undisturbed by passion" (*MFE* xiv). To read Goethe, and by implication to read in the fullest sense, was not a docile or passive undertaking but a full expression of agency. To garner the moral import of Goethe required "the power as life does." To read deeply is in this sense to live deeply. The "power" required for it is not only the strength of sympathetic comprehension but also the power of choosing and deciding. To read a novel may be to view a mirror of life, but that viewing was not, for Fuller, an alternative to life or a separation from it.

Fuller may have had Goethe's conception of the "Daimonic" (*Dämonische*) in mind as she discussed both his books and the state of mind necessary for reading them. Eckermann had recorded several important Goethean pronouncements on "that secret, problematical power, which all men feel, which no philosopher explains, and over which the religious help themselves with courageous words" (*MFE* 375). These provocative announcements held Fuller's strongest attention. Partaking of the mystery and power of divinity, the Daimonic is not itself divine or religious in any pietistic sense. It is, however, closely interwoven with, and indeed a necessary part of, the "creative activity" that Fuller had identified as Goethe's "law" (*MFE* xiii).[13] It is nevertheless a lawless kind of law, undeniably present but emphatically uncontrollable. "The Demoniacal is that which cannot be explained by Reason or Understanding," Goethe instructed Eckermann. "It lies not in my nature but I am subject to it." But when Eckermann probed deeper, asking if the Daimonic was in fact the devil, Goethe denied it. "Mephistopheles is too negative a being. The Demoniacal manifests itself in positive active power among artists; it is often found among musicians; more rarely among painters" (*MFE* 379). Fuller, who later wrote appreciatively on Beethoven, would surely have recognized the Daimonic force of music and its capability to sweep up the consciousness and the emotions.[14] This was, she believed, the kind of experience accessible in the deeply immersive experience of energized reading. For Fuller, literary analysis was closely associated with the deep, creative reading that Goethe's work enabled. Such experiences of literary absorption were essential elements of self-culture. Reading Goethe did not provide her with a set of ideas or principles to adopt as her own, but it engaged her in the difficult work of confronting and clarifying her own beliefs.

This conviction that literature was an entry into life, and not a substitute for it, informed her praise for Goethe as a great "observer" of both "human nature" and "external nature," an achievement that required both comprehension and judgment. Fuller called him the one who best understood her generation and what it confronted. "He has great delicacy of penetration, and a better tact at selecting objects than almost any who has looked at the time of which I am a child" (*MFE* xix). Not blinded by an abstraction or an unrealized future, Goethe could more clearly see the present.

Mutual Explanation

Fuller's translation of *Eckermann's Conversations*, with its sharp and rousing account of Goethe's unquestionable power and achievement, was a personal triumph, marking her as an authoritative presence on the Boston literary scene. It demonstrated not only her stature as a linguist but also her mastery of the literary essay, a largely male domain in the 1830s. With this volume she took a central place among the transcendentalists, confirming that literary critique stood with theological analysis as the movement's defining purposes. Shortly after the volume appeared, she began the first of her innovative public Conversations for women. These were signal events in the history of the American women's movement.[15] These Conversations broke through the deeply entrenched barrier between the male public sphere and the female domestic sphere, bringing women together for public discussion of literary and philosophical subjects and, most importantly, for discussion of the question of women's role in society. Held yearly through 1844, the Conversations provided the venue through which Fuller, as Zwarg writes, "articulated the association between conversation and feminist agency" (Zwarg 163). Here she was able to link the importance of focused reading and public discussion with her growing recognition of the control over women's self-development. Fuller drew from established forms of discourse such as the sermon and the increasingly popular lyceum in the Conversations, and they also had roots in important women's traditions—the European literary "salon" and a strong New England tradition of women's reading societies and female academies.

Fuller's exposure to the convention of the salon, a conversational gathering of intellectual and artistic figures often centered on a charismatic woman of taste and literary authority, originated in her reading of Germaine de Staël, the founder of a salon in eighteenth-century Switzerland and Paris. She wrote *Corinne; or Italy* (1807) and *Germany* (1810–1813), widely read works that had an enormous international impact and were key influences on the development of transcendentalism.[16] De Staël's influence on Fuller's literary ambitions, and on her sense of herself as a woman recognized for her intellectual capability, cannot be overestimated. De Staël was an exemplar of artistic taste, and as Ellen Moers has shown, a facilitator of interchange and friendship among her guests—"a talker and provoker of serious talk by others," who used "the salon as a medium of education or philosophical discussion." Her personal example was greatly magnified through her fictional character Corinne, who embodied a commanding myth of the "heroine" enacting her greatness through a variety of artistic and conversational means. "Poet, *improvisatrice*, dancer, actress, translator, musician, painter, singer, lecturer—Corinne is all of these, as well as a published author of various unspecified volumes," Moers notes. In the early nineteenth century, Corinne signified the rise of the female intellectual. Fuller was among many women, including Jane Austen, Jane Welsh Carlyle, Elizabeth Barrett Browning, George Sand, and Harriet Beecher Stowe, who were profoundly stirred by the possibilities exemplified in the myth of Corinne.[17] In her mentor Eliza Farrar, Fuller had experienced a woman with many of the qualities of a de Staël, an accomplished author and social catalyst among the talented and perceptive. Her adoption had played a crucial role in Fuller's struggle for an intellectual identity and had placed her in a position in which she could perform a Corinne-like role as a mesmerist, conversationalist, literary guide, and critical authority. With help from Elizabeth Palmer Peabody and Sophia Ripley to gather a group of knowledgeable Boston women, Fuller offered her first formal Conversation in Peabody's West Street Book Shop, a meeting place and discussion forum among the transcendentalists.[18]

Fuller's plans for the Conversations had evolved after her experience with Peabody and Bronson Alcott at the Temple School in Boston. Alcott, a close friend of Emerson's, was at the center of the transcendental ferment, aiming through his school to translate the movement's core faith in an inner-driven self-development into educational practice. By the standards of the day, his school was student-centered, open, and dialogic. Alcott attempted to bring ideas and analytical skills out of the students, rather than stuff information into them by repetition and rote memorization. Working with Alcott enabled Fuller to gain a more stable and much better-remunerated teaching position at the new Greene Street School in Providence, where she taught very successfully for a year and a half. Recent scholars have emphasized the importance of this stint in teaching to Fuller's development of principles of dialogue and collaboration, and the accounts of Fuller's students suggest that her classroom was indeed lively and challenging.[19]

Fuller's decision to hold her Conversations was linked very closely to the publication of her Eckermann book, as an archival discovery by Amanda Ritchie has shown. In 2001, Ritchie found that "Reading Journal O," an eleven-page manuscript among the Fuller papers in Harvard's Houghton Library, was actually not a "reading journal" at all but the record of a series of four smaller invited conversations that Fuller held in the spring and summer of 1839, before she launched the larger series in November of that year. This earlier "prototype," as Ritchie terms it, was undertaken almost simultaneously with the publication of her Eckermann translation in late May, and its central focus was on Goethe, expanding through him to a broader consideration of aesthetics.[20] Fuller's notation on her first Conversation group about Goethe is indicative of her commitment to reading, dialogue, and interchange as the operative means of creative activity. "I showed why people on first knowing [Goethe] undervalue his profoundest remarks because he never comes to impose or make a point, and you must see how one thing bears on another in his thought to appreciate him at all." Goethe's indirection or suggestiveness is, however, ultimately more powerful. "He will not let you stay in your own place but draws you to himself 'und fort und fort' [and onward and onward]." Yet in the end, Fuller observed, Goethe creates independent thinkers rather than disciples. "The very nature of his genius forbids your mingling in his stream" (Ritchie 217). Fuller's Conversations were well received, continuing in Boston for five winters (1839–1844), and the comments by Fuller's contemporaries suggest their success until the final lecture—the only one in which men were allowed to participate. Even though the men were supporters and admirers of Fuller such as Alcott and Emerson, they seem to have treated the occasion as a political argument, thereby spoiling the fragile atmosphere of mutuality and deep communication that Fuller had been able to cultivate. To the women who gathered for these Conversations, that atmosphere of mutual exchange was crucial.[21] Fuller walked the boundary between performance and intimacy in the Conversations, acting in part as a charismatic female intellectual—a Corinne—yet also as a caring midwife for a community forming itself around high, sympathetic thinking and its ethical and artistic expression. As Fuller made clear in a letter to Sophia Ripley, her goal was an interchange of ideas, in a forum that stimulated serious thought and open expression. She hoped to provide "a point of union to well-educated and thinking women in a city which, with great pretensions to mental refinement, boasts at present nothing of the kind." Fuller was ready, she assured Ripley, simply to suggest topics and lead the resulting dialogue, but she hoped for something more rigorous and systematic, "to pass in review the departments of thought and knowledge and endeavor to place them in due relation to one another in our minds." Such a challenge was vital in order "to systematize thought and give a precision in which our sex are so deficient, chiefly, I think because they have so few inducements to test and classify what they receive" (*FL* 2:86–87).

Fuller's hope that the Conversations might cultivate more systematic and critical thinking was at the heart of the feminist energy driving the project. She believed that gathering in open but focused discussion would help women "to ascertain what pursuits are best suited to us in our time and state of society, and how we may make best use of our means for building up the life of thought upon the life of action." This was a call for the critical interrogation of the male public sphere and the female domestic sphere—a critique of the foundations of patriarchal society. Fuller understood, of course, that to advertise the gatherings as political strategy sessions would doom their appeal and compromise their probable success. She also believed that subjects such as "the departments of thought and knowledge" or "literature and the arts present in endless profusion" (*FL* 2:87, 89) would inevitably lead a roomful of aware and educated women to consider "What were we born to do? How shall we do it?" (*FL* 2:87). Fuller felt that her efforts to establish herself as a thinking woman could benefit women who struggled inwardly with intellectual capabilities that had no outlet. "I can scarcely have felt the wants of others so much without feeling my own still more deeply," she confided to Ripley. "Such power as I have thus far exerted," she wrote, arose from "the depth of my feeling" (*FL* 2:87).

Fuller's intention to bring an awakening, both intellectual and political, through her Conversations are confirmed in Nancy Craig Simmons's 1994 edition of the only extant detailed account of the first series of twelve Conversations. The transcript is that of Elizabeth Palmer Peabody, written from an "abstract" that she prepared after each Conversation and completed later.[22] Peabody's record provides ample evidence of Fuller's focus "on woman-centered topics throughout," and supports the idea that both Fuller and her audience were resisting notions of male-female difference that "promote inequality," and were quite aware of "the concept of woman's 'sphere' as a cultural construction" (Simmons 196). Fuller's pursuit of a genuine dialogue with her audience was, it is important to note, part of this feminist program. "Miss Fuller guarded against the idea that she was to *teach* any thing," Peabody wrote. "She merely meant to be the nucleus of conversation," whose role was "to give her own best thoughts on any subject that was named, as a means of calling out the thoughts of others." Fuller could bring her audience to the difficult task of articulating their thoughts, the process that she believed was a crucial step in women's emergence into a public role. Fuller warned that "we should probably have to go through some mortification in finding how much less we knew than we thought—& on the other hand we should probably find ourselves encouraged by seeing how much & how rapidly we should gain by making simple & clear effort for expression" (Simmons 203). With this formula of advance through self-expression, Fuller brought the principle of self-culture to bear on the question of the roles and rights of women.

During the same winter when Fuller launched her first series of Conversations, Emerson was also lecturing in Boston on the "Present Age." As Phyllis Cole has noted, Emerson was slow to embrace the idea of political equality for women.[23] In this series, however, he contended that "nothing has more remarkably distinguished the Present Age than the great harvest of projects it has yielded for the reform of domestic, social, civil, literary, and ecclesiastical institutions."[24] His placement of "domestic" reforms at the head of this list was not accidental. The reform of the household, of marriage, of child rearing, of education, of vocation, of patterns of spending and consumption were fundamental to any major redirection of modern society, he believed. As Fuller insisted, these reforms absolutely required an expansion of the role of women in society. Emerson defined the present age as a struggle between "the party of the Past and the party of the Future" (*EEL* 3:187), two ever-present poles of society that struggle for ascendency. At this distinctive moment, he thought that "men have been animated with a faith in the Soul" which has given "the whole of modern history ... an ethical character" (*EEL* 3:188). These terms are quite consonant with Fuller's insistence that women must defy any code or institution that denies them the fullest self-development and self-expression. One of the defining changes of the present age, she believed, was the demand of women to claim their inherent capabilities and put them to use.

Elective Affinities

Fuller's Conversations continued into the mid-1840s, influencing a generation of women and making her the founding philosophical voice of the American women's movement.[25] These years were, for Fuller, a period of dizzying intellectual expansion that included her editorship of *The Dial*, her experimentation in fiction, poetry, and travel writing, and her conceptualization of the political and philosophical case for women's rights. These new pursuits emerged with her continuance as Goethe's defender and advocate. Shortly after Fuller's *Eckermann's Conversations with Goethe* appeared in 1839, the *Christian Examiner* published a review of John Sullivan Dwight's edition of *Select Minor Poems of Goethe and Schiller*, which had also appeared in George Ripley's Specimens of Foreign Standard Literature series.[26] A young Unitarian minister with decided transcendentalist leanings, Dwight would soon join the Ripleys' Brook Farm commune and eventually become America's most influential classical music critic.[27] Dwight had done most of the translations in the volume, but he had also invited several others, including Fuller, to contribute to the book. One of the other contributing translators, George Bancroft, was the reviewer for the *Christian Examiner*, and he used the occasion to applaud Ripley and Dwight and to launch a caustic attack on Goethe, a man with "no philosophy, no creed, no principles."[28] While Bancroft did not refer directly to Fuller, or to her Eckermann volume, he was aware of its recent publication. Bancroft was a formidable figure. He sailed to Göttingen with Frederic Henry Hedge in 1818 to study languages, biblical criticism, and philological methods and studied in Berlin and Heidelberg. In his travels he met Wilhelm von Humboldt, Friedrich Schleiermacher, and Goethe. By the time that his attack on Goethe appeared, he had already launched the multivolume *History of the United States of America* which would secure his fame as a historian. He was at the beginnings of a political career that would bring him into President Polk's cabinet in the 1840s. With a significant investment in its culture, Bancroft was careful not to attack Germany itself. He made a strong distinction between the unprincipled Goethe and the admirable Schiller, "a purer writer and a nobler man," whose "genius was kindled with the divine light" (Bancroft 373).

Bancroft's essay was amplified in importance when the Harvard scholar Cornelius Conway Felton brought out a translation of Wolfgang Menzel's *German Literature* in 1840 in Ripley's Specimens series. Felton was a distinguished classicist and linguist, who later served as president of Harvard

(1860–1862), but his place in literary history was fixed when Van Wyck Brooks labeled him "the anti-Transcendentalist" in his influential study *The Flowering of New England* (1936).²⁹ Before the threat of transcendentalism had seemed imminent, Felton had declared the Weimar of Schiller, Wieland, and others "the Athens of Modern Europe," the highest praise that a classicist could bestow.³⁰ In a glowing review of Goethe's *Iphigenia in Tauris*, Felton praised Goethe's perceptive treatment of his classical material, only "a single item in a long list of claims which Goethe may assert to the intellectual supremacy of continental Europe" (Felton 191). Goethe's "unrivalled versatility" was the basis of this assertion. "He possessed, what belongs to the most gifted minds, the power of entering into, and identifying himself completely with every mode and phasis of human life" (Felton 188). In emphasizing Goethe's capacity for universal understanding, Felton identified the trait that had become so central to Fuller's appreciation of him. Felton, however, made a dramatic shift of opinion, following Menzel, in berating Goethe as an unpatriotic cosmopolitan and dilettante. More importantly, he attacked Goethe's moral character, arguing that his literary portrayal of female characters seemed to be only a form of flattery whose aim was to attract women. Menzel's assault on Goethe's morality added support to Bancroft's recent condemnation, increasing the alarm about the frankness with which Goethe portrayed sexuality and infidelity, particularly in the novel *Elective Affinities* (*Wahlverwandschaften*).³¹ This was the book that Fuller deemed Goethe's most commanding and morally discerning work.

These castigations seared Fuller, who had portrayed Goethe as the master builder not just of literary characters but of human character itself. Having assumed the editorship of *The Dial*, she now had a venue for response. She launched an incisive counterattack that began with a blistering dismantling of Menzel. Felton is nowhere mentioned in the essay, but Fuller's outraged denunciation of Menzel would no doubt have stung him, after he had labored through a three-volume translation of Menzel's key work. Merging her title with her first line for maximum impact, Fuller declared that "Menzel's View of Goethe is that of a Philistine" whose perspective is severely limited and whose taste and aesthetic judgment are corrupted.³² Menzel, she argued, was simply incapable of judging Goethe, unable of reading "the prophet by the light of his own law." Conceding that Menzel had "a vigorous and brilliant mind, and a wide, though imperfect culture," she nevertheless portrayed him as a man attempting to measure a mountain with a yardstick. "He is a man of talent, but talent cannot comprehend genius." As Fuller insisted, Goethe was an era maker, "a prophet of our own age, as well as a representative of his own" (MFMenzel 340). At stake here was the capacity to claim and to guide modernity, to define the condition of the present age and the one to come. She recognized in Felton and Bancroft, and in most of the resistance to Goethe, a reactionary attitude that was poison to human creativity and human progress. Whatever Goethe's personal faults may have been, his great achievement lay in his capacity for aspiration, a quality under threat in the attitude of his critics. She pointed to Goethe's poem "The Godlike" ("Das Göttliche") as an expression of the core of his achievement, a call on men and women to become the "Type of those loftier / Beings of whom the heart whispers" (MFMenzel 345).

Goethe's creed of unceasing aspiration to a nobler life answered a generation that had lost its bearing and empowered him to perform "his office of artist-critic to the then chaotic world of thought in his country." Despite the bitter opposition that he met, he was actually a bringer of order, Fuller believed. His cosmopolitan understanding, a "power of poetical sympathy to know every situation" (MFMenzel 342), protected him from ideological or aesthetic rigidity and enabled a kind of Olympian balance in his sensibility. This, in her own inner struggles, Fuller craved. "His serenity alone, in such a time of skepticism and sorrowful seeking, gives him a claim to all our study" (MFMenzel 346). This sentence alone clarifies much of Goethe's hold on Fuller. She was still torn by a poisonous mixture of grief, guilt, longing, and bitterness toward her father. By the time she wrote her final essays on Goethe, her emotional life had been further distressed by the unraveling of a set of friendships that had become an important source of sustenance. Goethe had come to represent more than the creative urge for her but rather an achievement of balance and "serenity" that she herself desired. She attributed Goethe's seeming tranquility to a "calm self-trust" which allowed him to move ever ahead without hesitation or regret. Her portrait of him, a projection of her own aspirations, captured a certainty that she sought. "He never halts, never repines, never is puzzled, like other men; that tranquility, full of life, that ceaseless but graceful motion, 'without haste, without rest,' for which we all are striving, he has attained." But even in Goethe, she acknowledged, something is absent. "Yes, yes, but I still doubt. 'Tis true, he says all this in a thousand beautiful forms, but he does not warm, he does not inspire me. In his certainty is no bliss, in his hope no love, in his faith no glow" (MFMenzel 346). Goethe's powerful intellect, even his command of the making of beauty, could not compensate for a void, and a chill, that curbed the impact of his work. Fuller longs for a missing ardor in her composed teacher Goethe and, by implication, in her beloved friend Emerson. This moment of admission, almost confessional, signaled Fuller's hard-won attainment of a new self-possession, a clearer grasp not only of the limits of her mentors but of her own needs and strengths as well.

Felton's objections, while aimed at Goethe's reputation, were more easily dismissed than those of Bancroft, who gave voice to the inflammatory concern about Goethe's portrayal of desire, courtship, and marriage, condemning *Elective Affinities*. This was the book that Fuller deemed Goethe's most powerful—and most highly moral—work. Bancroft's denunciation thus added painfully to her burden of Goethe's defense, raising questions about her championing of such a potentially harmful author. Fuller's essay "Goethe" in the July 1841 *Dial* was not only her most comprehensive assessment of his achievement but also a spirited defense of the censured *Elective Affinities* as a masterpiece.[33] "For myself, I have never felt more completely that the very thing which genius should always make us feel, that I was in its circle, and could not get out till its spell was done, and its last spirit permitted to depart" (MFGoethe 33–34). But her impassioned defense of Goethe also signaled her graduation from his tutelage. She began by acknowledging her sense of Goethe's "coldness," which she now understood as "an intellect . . . too much developed in proportion to the moral nature" (MFGoethe 2). This seems at first a concession to Goethe's adversaries, but Fuller quickly turned this into a sign of Goethe's brilliance. "Pardon him, World, that he was too Worldly. Do not wonder, Heart, that he was so heartless. Believe, Soul, that one so true, as far as he went, must yet be initiated into the deeper mysteries of the Soul" (MFGoethe 3). These pleas echo Fuller's own striving for approval and self-acceptance. Her faith is that a sympathetic and aesthetically sensitive reading of Goethe's work, especially his most controversial novel, would be a redemptive act both for the resistant reader and for Goethe's legacy. Such sympathetic understanding, here advanced as a principle of interpretive reading, became the guiding principle of her work as she moved from questions of literature to those of social justice.

"Perhaps even now [Goethe] sees that we must accept limitations, only to transcend them," she wrote. As Goethe's reader, Fuller has freed herself and also freed his truth. "I seem to see his soul," she wrote, "wingless, motionless, unable to hide from itself any subterfuge of labor," repeating now "the simple words he would never directly say on earth—God beyond Nature—Faith beyond Sight—the Seeker nobler than the Meister" (MFGoethe 3). Goethe unmasked is no longer a master but a kindred thinker whose limits have helped to reveal his wisdom. This transcendental Goethe is the "Seeker," now released through the work of sympathy. Fuller had seen *Elective Affinities* as the greatest and most challenging of Goethe's works. It put questions of marriage, sexuality, the responsibilities of women and men on clear display, leaving clear answers unstated.

The central figure, Ottilie (anglicized as Ottilia in Fuller's essay), exemplifies the bright promise of life for a young woman. Fuller recognized that Ottilie was the instrument through which Goethe expressed this interpretive sympathy. A "being of exquisite purity," she embodied "intellect and character . . . harmonized in feminine beauty" (MFGoethe 32). The structural weight of *Elective Affinities*, a novel in which ideas and characters vie for control, falls squarely on Ottilie. Later critics have confirmed Fuller's recognition of her centrality, and her complexity, noting her "improbably wide range of being"[34] and the sense in which she functions as "the vehicle of a Goethean faith" and "an expression of [Goethe's] creative ethical sensibility."[35] Ottilie is the youngest of four characters involved in a "love quadrangle" through which Goethe attempts to explore the application of the chemical law of "elective affinities" to human conduct.[36] A student of natural history himself, Goethe had taken a keen interest in the development of this theory and was, as Jeremy Adler has explained, deeply knowledgeable about the work of the scientists who had established, extended, and modified this theory in the eighteenth century. As Adler puts it, *Elective Affinities* was a query into "whether human life is governed by chemical laws." Recognizing the power of chemical "affinities" to decompose and reconstruct formations of matter, Goethe posited that such irresistible forces also accounted for human desire, bonding, abandonment, and re-bonding. Indeed, as Adler observes, the novel pursued the notion that both the natural world and the world of human emotions manifested the same "central 'idea' of affinity, in the way that all plants manifested the archetypal form of the leaf."[37] This notion itself was enough to ignite critics like Felton and Bancroft, since a superficial application of the theory to Goethe's dark and compelling narrative would seem to normalize erotic "affinities" as universal laws. Never reluctant to shock the conventional, Goethe also created a "constant undercurrent of sexuality and implicit sexual awareness" in the narrative, intensifying its capacity to mesmerize and alarm the reader.[38] It is hard to imagine that he could have succeeded so well without the pure and gentle Ottilie as his central character.

The plot's love quadrangle emerges when the orphaned Ottilie arrives as a younger addition to the household of her aunt Charlotte and Charlotte's husband, Eduard, a landed aristocrat. Shortly before Ottilie's arrival they also agree to host Eduard's close friend, known as the Captain, to assist them in planning a series of improvements to the estate. One senses Goethe's feel for the marriage-based conventions of the novel in the arrival of these new additions to the seemingly secure domestic arrangements at Eduard's estate. The bachelor Captain might well seem a satisfying romantic match for the pure-hearted Ottilie, and the two couples could form strong, mutually enriching domestic bonds. But here the laws of chemistry seem to intervene. Charlotte and the Captain, both pragmatic and project-oriented souls, find much to like in each other. And Eduard, who seems to have a generous portion of the passionate sensibility of Goethe's Werther, becomes enraptured with the self-effacing Ottilie.

This crossing of affinities is itself enough to establish Goethe's worrisome thesis that natural laws act beyond accepted moral codes to dictate the nature of emotional attraction and sexual drive. *Elective Affinities* has of course been recognized as Goethe's wry contribution to the nineteenth-century discourse on marriage, and Fuller was aware of this somewhat subversive element of the book. Rejecting the demand that an author must provide periodic "declarations of sentiment" and "lard his work here and there with ejaculations of horror and surprise" (MFGoethe 32) to guide the reader, she praised Goethe for his straightforward "discussion of the validity of the marriage vow." This issue makes "society tremble to its foundation" (MFGoethe 31).

Fuller does not mention Goethe's inclusion of one remarkable bedroom scene in *Elective Affinities* which proves to be the most consequential event in the novel. Known in the critical literature as "the act of spiritual adultery," or the "adultery in the marriage bed" (Plenderleith 407), it is a scene in which Eduard and Charlotte engage in sexual intercourse, with Eduard fantasizing about Ottilie and Charlotte about the Captain. The union results in the birth of a child, Otto, who has the facial features of the Captain and the eyes of Ottilie. Desire in this case seems to overpower physical laws, making known the inner wishes of both Eduard and Charlotte. But it is Ottilie, ironically, who becomes bound to the child, serving as Otto's constant attendant, and eventually bearing the burden of guilt for the accident that leads to his drowning. She thus becomes the guilty innocent, the victim of Eduard's misdirected love, which she has returned in a chaste and trusting way. Realizing the full consequences of these relationships, Ottilie withdraws utterly after the child's death into a severe penance, practicing an absolute renunciation of the world that brings on her sorrowful death through starvation.

Was Eduard's love misdirected by an inescapable elective affinity? Was Ottilie's response inevitable? Is morality possible in a world shaped essentially by unyielding laws? Goethe raises these questions, but as the critical response to the novel suggests, he does not fully answer them.[39] The wisdom of the novel lies in that deferral, which renders these unanswered questions more urgent. Fuller was wise enough to let those questions resonate for the reader, focusing instead on what she recognized as the book's central insight, the tragic waste of Ottilie's life. Fuller is less concerned about Ottilie's choices in the novel—her earlier responses to Eduard or her later disavowal of the world—than with the set of circumstances that develop around her. Through no fault of her own, she comes to realize that abandoning life is her only acceptable option for living. Goethe's greatest achievement might be explained as his success in making us respect the nobility of Ottilie's decision, grounded in a determination not to violate her own moral integrity. Ottilie's situation was, Fuller believed, one that many women shared. Goethe's penetrating realization of the characters, his representation of their self-sustaining existence as separate and authentic beings, confirmed his imaginative power to re-create life itself. "I was not carried away, instructed, delighted more than by other works, but I was there, living there." The characters of the novel, particularly Ottilie, were living others, persons whom we as readers must acknowledge as fellow women and men, both like us yet also entirely of themselves. As Fuller put it, they "live too intensely to let us live in them" (MFGoethe 34), and thus they demand the kind of interchange that expresses a recognition of and respect for their veracity and distinctiveness. She found Ottilie a figure surpassing all other literary creations in her authenticity. "Not even in Shakespeare have I so felt the organizing power of genius," she declared. "Through dead words I find the least gestures of this person, stamping themselves on my memory, betraying to the heart the secret of her life, which she herself, like all these divine beings, knew not" (MFGoethe 33). Ottilie is, in this sense, more than a literary character.

These lifelike qualities may have, in the view of its critics, added to the novel's dangers, but for Fuller this engaging authenticity made *Elective Affinities* "a work especially what is called moral in its outward effect, and religious even to piety in its spirit." Its moral center, Ottilie, is a "being of exquisite purity, with intellect and character so harmonized in feminine beauty, as they never before were found in any portrait of a woman painted by the hand of man." Fuller's "man" in this case is not wholly universal or without gender. Her claim is that Goethe, as a man, had understood women's ethical and spiritual aspirations, and had embodied them in Ottilie.

He had put those aspirations on trial in a world marked by "a sadness, as of an irresistible fatality brooding over the whole" (MFGoethe 32).

Into this world Ottilie, "too fair for vice, too finely wrought even for error, comes lonely, intense, and pale, like the evening star on a cold wintry night" (MFGoethe 32). A tragic heroine, Ottilie was also an emblem of the potential of the modern woman. Perhaps her deepest significance lay in the intersection of her capacity for growth and fulfillment and her tragic fate, an impact that Fuller explained in this resonant sentence: "I see not only what she was, but what she might have been, and live with her in yet untrodden realms" (MFGoethe 33). Few passages in the literature of the transcendentalist movement capture the aspirational, hope-centered spirit of the movement as well as this. Goethe's embodiment of a profound moral nature in Ottilie was a promise, and Ottilie's exemplary female nature was a ground for hope. Fuller saw her not simply as a particular woman but as an emblem of a world in which her virtues can live and thrive.

She had the capacity, even in her death, to bring something new into the world, to suggest the enduring accessibility of the "yet untrodden realms" of experience.

CHAPTER 3

"The Intelligent Freedom of the Universe"

"The Friend I Seek"

Fuller's embrace of Goethe's Ottilie as the emblem of women's oppression was an important step in her gradual recovery after her father's death. Her path to healing included her year of teaching at the Greene Street School in Providence, a position that paid well but exhausted her and kept her from the Boston cultural scene. In 1839 she moved with her family to Jamaica Plain, just south of Boston, a decision that, as Charles Capper notes, opened many important opportunities (Capper 1:257–58). This move assured her that she had escaped the choking isolation that began with her life in Groton and deepened after her father's death. In Boston she could recover the aesthetic stimulation vital to her balance, wellness, and imaginative growth. The friendships and conversations she craved were there.

Fuller's return was impressive. Arriving in April of 1839, she published her *Conversations with Goethe* in May and launched the first of her public Conversations for women in November. She also began to develop a group of friends as an integral component of her self-reconstruction. No one was more impressed with her than Emerson, who by the late 1830s had become the defining spokesman of transcendentalism. As he remembered, Fuller seemed "rich in friends, rich in experiences, rich in culture" (*Memoirs*

1:204), possessing a charm that captivated him. Fuller remembered one of his wryly self-deprecating observations about their differences. "He says: 'I come to him as the European to the Hindoo, or as the gay Trouvere to the Puritan in his steeple hat'" (*FL* 6:337). She had closely followed Emerson's rise to prominence in the early 1830s, attracted by his rare form of spirituality and his intellectual rebelliousness. Approaching him as an aspiring friend when they met in 1836, she charmed him and essentially began to remake him, or so he felt. She playfully coaxed him out of his scholarly shell, he remembered, with eyes that "swam with fun and drolleries, and the very tides of joy and superabundant life" (*Memoirs* 1:203). As their friendship and mutual respect accelerated in the late 1830s, they faced the question of the bounds of their friendship. She recognized his originality of mind and his impatience with social conventions. She was also aware that Emerson in turn recognized her "rich & brilliant genius" (*JMN* 16:94). Drawn to his openness to new thinking, she sought him as a mentor and a confidant, and as it sometimes seems from their correspondence, something more as well.

Despite his reserve, Emerson craved friendships based on frank intellectual exchange. His 1841 essay "Friendship," shaped largely by his conversations with Fuller, has only recently taken a prominent place in the Emerson canon as a counterpoint to his well-known hymn to "Self-Reliance."[1] "No law can be sacred to me but that of my nature," he declared in "Self-Reliance." "I awoke this morning with devout thanksgiving for my friends, the old and the new," he countered in "Friendship" (*CW* 2:30, 114). The desire for companionship also developed among others drawn to transcendental thought, resulting in a rich literary discourse on the importance of friendship. This included not just Emerson's "Friendship" but Thoreau's fervent meditation on friendship in *A Week on the Concord and Merrimack Rivers*, Fuller's bold analysis of marriage in *Woman in the Nineteenth Century*, and her brilliant and moving letters to Emerson and Caroline Sturgis in 1839–1841.[2] All these powerful statements reveal a longing for closer and more authentic relationships and show the frustrating complexities of achieving them. Perhaps the best expressions of this hunger for association were in the realm of personal letters and journals and in the private conversations now lost to us. Fuller's achievement and influence as an author and activist cannot be understood without attention to her ardent quest for deep conversation and open friendship.

Fuller and Emerson saw that they could learn from each other and that they faced, in some cases, similar problems. Christina Zwarg has given us the most searching account of the basis of their relationship, emphasizing how the utopian doctrines of Charles Fourier provided a framework that made their letters and conversations exploratory and aspirational. They felt that a dramatic cultural shift was underway, and they regarded each other as representatives of this newness. Although their occasional visits were important, theirs was a friendship based on the exchange of letters, the writing of which was, for both, an exercise of genuine bonding and high literary endeavor. As Zwarg explains, Fuller's letters enhanced Emerson's "*desire* to write" and thereby fostered "a sense of experiment" (Zwarg 34), opening him to a wider range of thought than books alone could provide. There was also, clearly, an electricity between them. Emerson's "warm, highly personalized, and often flirtatious" (Zwarg 41) letters to Fuller differed widely from his public lectures. Such open conversational exchange helped him to achieve the stylistic leap that we find in *Essays: First Series* (1841), the book in which Emerson made his mark as an innovative master of the essay. The magnetism of his essays' intermingled voices, their pull of impassioned sincerity, their shockingly abrupt shifts of tone, and the sumptuous metaphors of works such as "Self-Reliance" and "Circles" were generated in some measure by his correspondence with Fuller.

Such close intimacy did not come easily for Emerson. Fuller believed that Emerson kept much of his genius suppressed and regarded this as a flaw of character as well as a hindrance to his literary craft. She pushed Emerson hard to open up. As she cultivated her friendship with Emerson, she also brought three charismatic and imaginative young people into a circle of strong mutual affection. In October 1838 she sent him a packet of letters from Samuel Ward, Anna Barker, and Caroline Sturgis as enticement to the possibilities of dedicated and noble friendships. Deep friendship can be a thrilling and inspirational thing, she suggested, and the young can perhaps teach us something about it.

Emerson's interested response to the letters is revealing in the way that it established the grounds of his developing dialogue with Fuller. I love the idea of friendship, she seemed to say, but its workings are always disheartening. Writing to her in response, he declared, "I begin to be proud of my contemporaries & wish to behold their whole course." His enthusiasm, however, was impeded by his uncertainty about intense social involvement. "We are armed all over with these subtle antagonisms which as soon as we meet begin to play, & translate all poetry into such stale prose! It seems to me that almost all people *descend* somewhat into society." As Emerson saw it, the allure of the relationship almost always fails us because "all association must be a compromise." Neither party in a friendship can fully express themselves, and both become disillusioned. "The very flower & aroma of the flower of each of the beautiful natures disappears as they approach each other." Emerson is guarding his privacy with this response and also providing a rationale for the distraction-proof solitude that he had found necessary for thinking and writing. As his outpouring to Fuller continued, however, it began to change in tone, becoming a plea for some new and positive way to understand falling into a friendship. "What a perpetual disappointment is actual society even of the virtuous & gifted. I think they can never do justice to themselves or to each other." The "they" that Emerson mentions are presumably Fuller's attractive young friends. But implicitly "they" are also Fuller and Emerson, who aspire to ennobling "society" but wonder if they can attain that ideal. Despite his worries, Emerson did not turn Fuller's offering away. He was frank in his initial skepticism—so forcefully frank that readers of his letter may miss his acknowledgment of Fuller's leadership in a grand exploration of the boundaries of friendships. Having asserted that even "the virtuous and gifted" cannot do one another "justice," Emerson closed with a gesture of appreciative openness. "Well, the more precious to me is this intimation this prophecy of finer relations in the deeps of beautiful nature."[3] I remain open. I hope for the best.

Their friendship continued to develop within the framework of their connections with Ward, Barker, and Sturgis. The overlapping bonds among this bright and discerning quintet were intense and carried elements of romantic attraction and sublimated erotic desire. As Emerson recalled,

Fuller "extorted the secret of life which cannot be told without setting heart & mind in a glow, & thus had the best of those she saw. Whatever romance, whatever virtue, whatever impressive experience—this came to her, and she lived in a superior circle.... She was perfectly true to this confidential trust. She never confounded relations but kept a hundred fine threads in her hand without crossing or entangling any. Total intimacy" (*JMN* 11:495).

Fuller's gift was to regard her friends as if their inner lives were both sacred and compelling. She brought them out of themselves so that she could, paradoxically, affirm the primacy and wonder of their inmost souls. The energy of transcendentalism radiated from the trust that the inner life was inherently holy. The group became perhaps less a "circle" of friends than a network of overlapping friendships that were each evolving simultaneously, with consequences for all. Fuller was the center of the group, working as a kind of medium among them. She used the charisma of the younger trio to coax Emerson out of his practiced aloofness. She used him as an intellectual touchstone, recognizing his extraordinary prescience with emerging ideas that gave him magnetic authority with the young. Fuller was also drawn to Emerson as a supportive confidant, one who could help her restore herself after the shocks of her early life. She certainly recognized his soundly married rectitude and was in any case deeply attracted to Sam Ward. She was galvanized by Emerson's intellectual depth and integrity and his remarkable literary gift, traits she had previously encountered only in books. She aspired to be a close and intimate friend *to* him and also aspired *for* him, recognizing the still untapped capacities and sensibilities that he seemed reluctant to explore. She believed that she could help him find them.

Fuller's budding friendship with Emerson paralleled her romantic fixation on Ward, the notable young man who became the catalyst of a complex interpersonal drama among the quintet. Fuller met Ward in 1835 through Eliza Farrar and came to know him better in 1838 after he had returned from a post-graduation European tour. Ward's nascent artistic talent had been ignited by his European travels, and he had brought home numerous reproductions of the works of the Renaissance masters. Fuller was impressed with his taste and earnest interest in the arts (he would later become a founder of the Metropolitan Museum of Art), and she and Emerson eagerly studied these works. They saw in Ward a forward-looking sign of an awakening America. Fuller's feeling for Ward, however, went beyond his artistic tastes. As Bell Gale Chevigny aptly puts it, Fuller and Ward "fell into an exuberant intimacy" (Chevigny 108), a condition short of a romantic bond but strong enough to give Fuller hope for that.[4] Fuller offered Ward important approval as a man of artistic discernment at a moment when he was struggling with the possibilities of art as a vocation. To Fuller, his sensibility made him an example of a new kind of masculinity that could express itself creatively and artistically. Fuller's nurturing of his artistic inclinations thus became, at least for her, a masked courtship. In a letter to Caroline Sturgis, Fuller described her circle as an idealized family group, in which the younger Caroline and Anna Barker would be "two alone I would have held by the hand," along with "Mr E for the representative of religious aspiration and one other of Earth's beauty I thought my circle would be as complete as friendship could make it" (FL 2:93). That "one other," who represented beauty, was Ward. At the center of this imagined friendship family, playing roles that were sisterly, maternal, and seductive, Fuller was both fully engaged and fulfilled. Jason Hoppe has helped us understand that Fuller's pleasure in this reconstituted family circle was magnified by her conception of the group in profoundly artistic terms. It was as if a rapturously melodic sonata played by five talented and affectionate companions were constantly being performed. Fuller was both a performer and the conductor of this group, and the delicate balance of personalities among them was to her a still developing masterpiece. Fuller's friends meant for her an idealized or typological character, Hoppe shows, that in some senses transcended their actual presence, making their places in her friendship circle both inevitable and irreplaceable.[5]

Ward was flattered by Fuller's attention. Her associations with both Farrar and Emerson bolstered her stature and added weight to her encouragement, as did her command of German literature and her engagement with serious scholarship and translation. Ward's sincere respect and gratitude could not, however, be translated into the kind of ardent rapport that Fuller sought. In 1987 Eleanor M. Tilton published an article based on her research on Ward's still preserved letters to his family in the late 1830s. Tilton found that Ward and Anna Barker had become romantically attached immediately after they met at Interlaken in Switzerland in August 1837, well before Fuller developed her infatuation with Ward. Fuller's impassioned response to Ward's kindness and courtesies was, Tilton writes, a damaging "self-deception."[6] When Fuller finally realized that Ward would marry Anna Barker, she was shattered.[7] She sent him a sizzling letter in late September of 1839 that began "You love me no more," and continued with accusation and anguish. "How did you pray me to draw near to you! What words were spoken in impatience of separation! How did you promise to me, aye, and doubtless to yourself, too, of all we might be to one another" (FL 2:90). This was the deepest emotional distress Fuller had suffered since the death of her father. Its pain was multiplied because her love for Ward was tightly interwoven with the friendship group she had assembled around her. That circle had given her a new identity and sense of well-being.[8] This experiment in intimate friendship had been her refuge from loneliness, and as it began to evaporate, Fuller was pushed into recurrent agony.

She hoped for support and perhaps for a more intimate friendship with Emerson. "I like no deep stakes," he warned her in one letter, as she pushed him for more in their correspondence. "I am a coward at gambling—I will bask in the common sun a while longer" (EL 2:240). That Emerson could go only so far into deep emotional entanglement with Fuller was not, as he saw it, an end to their friendship. But his attitude stymied her search for a reliable source of absolute support and accord. Still stung by Ward's betrayal, Fuller began to enumerate the difficulties that kept her apart from Emerson. "Mr. E scarce knows the instincts," she wrote, "and uses them rather for rejection than reception when he uses them at all" (FL 2:161). The feeling that Emerson was fixed in an unchangeable posture frustrated Fuller immensely. He made her feel that she sought a trivial game of emotions, toying with moods rather than an earnest search for mutual self-understanding. He made her feel, too, as if she had to rise to a level of gravity that he had already attained. This was not highbrow snobbishness; Emerson had made it clear that he had learned much from her and saw her as an equal in their intellectual exchange. It was, as she began to recognize, that Emerson did not value what she deemed essential, a close and supportive companionship in creative thought that could nourish and broaden both partners. Emerson wanted to exchange and consider ideas and conceptions with her. She insisted on working together with him in mutual discovery. "In friendship with R. W. E., I cannot hope to feel that I am his or he is mine. He has nothing peculiar, nothing sacred for his friend" (*FL* 2:161), she wrote. We miss her point if we take this "peculiar" or "sacred" thing in romantic or erotic terms. Zwarg has rightly noted that there was a current of repressed desire between them, but at this moment a gesture toward the physical by either of them was unthinkable and would have arrested their relationship instantly.

Fuller moved closer to their differences. "He speaks of a deed, of a thought to any commoner as much as to his peer. His creed is, show thyself, let them take as much as they can" (*FL* 2:161). Fuller began to recognize that this was less an intentional effort to distance himself from her personally than a fundamental disparity in belief or values between them. Emerson feared friendship as a barrier, a potential distraction to the principled focus on the pursuit of truth. Close friendship may divert the individual from his or her natural or intended path, he believed. It can diminish the self rather than enlarge it. Fuller continued with a perceptive observation on the impact of this attitude. "His friendship is only strong preference and he weighs and balances, buys and sells you and himself all the time" (*FL* 2:161). This would be an utterly damning description of Emerson as a cold manipulator of others were it not for Fuller's phrase "and himself." What she had discovered was Emerson's distrust of the interpersonal as an access to ultimate truth.

Later, in a letter of September 21, 1840, Fuller enlarged these observations into a blistering missive confronting Emerson about the condition of their friendship. This and several other letters to Emerson and Caroline Sturgis are among the best examples of Fuller's brilliant writing. Since her historical recovery in the late twentieth century, her dazzling prose has been overlooked among her extraordinary list of achievements. It is difficult to classify these and many other letters and journals as literature, given their intimately personal context and the strong emotions they reveal. Nevertheless, they must be recognized for their creativity, adept expression, incisive thought, and forceful impact on the reader—the values that typify great literary accomplishment. Her letter of September 29 made clear to Emerson her sense of being misused, her emotional exhaustion, and her growing anger. Emerson's "light," she told him, "will never understand my fire," his "clear eye will never discern the law by which I am filling my circle," and his "simple force will never interpret my need of manifold being" (FL 2:159). Fuller merged painful loss with searing accusation, pleading with Emerson as she also reproached him. The letter anticipated *Woman in the Nineteenth Century* in its portrayal of the awakening female recognition of the male denial of women's equal standing. Fuller passionately declared women's equality and dignity. "I have felt the impossibility of meeting far more than you," she wrote, telling Emerson that her patient "abiding" had been "strong proof that we are to be much to one another." Emerson, however, had failed to understand her effort to unite with him, thus denying the sacredness of friendship itself. He had not recognized the holy path she had taken toward her healing, which she had hoped would be a shared quest for mutual self-illumination. "If you have not seen this stair on which God has been so untiringly leading me to himself, you have indeed been wholly ignorant of me" (FL 2:160).

Fuller's effort to know Emerson, and to allow him to know her, had not been willfully possessive but was a call for support from a man who professed spiritual wisdom and guidance. "Did you not then see what was meant by this crying for the moon?" she demanded, mockingly condemning his impassive responses as a frigid dismissal. He had said, "I know not what this means; perhaps this will trouble me; the time will come when I shall hide my eyes from this mood." This account of Emerson's rigidity led Fuller to a disheartening conclusion. "You are not the friend I seek" (FL 2:160). She sought a friendship in which each person must come to a state of acknowledgment—actively knowing and openly being known—to generate productive mutuality. Fuller's frustration with Emerson was that she could not find a way to enable him to understand her view of experience. To see through her eyes would not nullify his own perspective, she believed, but it would provide a bridge of exchange, a mutual acknowledgment that could enrich them both. She had learned from him, and she believed strongly that he could learn from her. She saw more in him than a rebelling Unitarian minister. There was a poet, an artist in him that she hoped to release. He seemed, however, to fear that Fuller might lead him away from the remarkably productive path he had followed as a lecturer and an author, or she might disrupt the balance of his studious routines. Whatever his reasons for rejecting her, he could not satisfactorily explain them to Fuller. Even so, he urged Fuller not to walk away from their friendship.

Two weeks after the Ward-Barker marriage, Fuller responded gratefully to a supportive letter from Caroline Sturgis, the person who best understood her agony. "Your recognition, my Caroline, added to the happiness it could not deepen.—Rightly you say that the past distrust was always forgiven by me as it is now by yourself" (*FL* 2:163). The importance of her use of the word "recognition" cannot be overlooked, given her demanding letter to Emerson. It also suggests Sturgis's important role in Fuller's redirection in the early 1840s. Their newly energized friendship allowed Fuller to begin regaining her emotional and intellectual momentum. Fuller found the perceptive and articulate Sturgis a stimulating, even challenging correspondent. Emerson had also found the same. In his 1995 *Emerson: Mind on Fire*, Robert D. Richardson notes that Emerson showed unusual receptiveness to Sturgis's "verve, charm, lyric grace, and a kind of literary coquettishness" in her letters."[9] At the age of twenty, Sturgis was exchanging letters with two of the most eloquent figures of the age. Sturgis's open-mindedness and her self-portrayal as an unsettled inquirer particularly attracted Fuller.

In a letter of October 22, 1840, one of Fuller's most complex and penetrating pieces, she struggled to explain her anguished state to Sturgis. Although she has been only slightly acknowledged as a marginal figure in the long historiography of transcendentalism, Sturgis's importance in the movement's discourse on friendship has recently brought her into clearer focus. As Kathleen Lawrence notes, "Fuller and Sturgis came to love one another deeply, in spite of friction between their two powerful and independent natures."[10] Fuller's letter to Sturgis seems in part an internal debate in which she both denied and welcomed the abandonment she felt in the collapse of the friendship circle. "I cannot plunge into myself enough. I cannot dedicate myself sufficiently. The life that flows in upon me from so many quarters is too beautiful to be checked" (*FL* 2:167). This is a testimony of a powerful new enlightenment that Fuller had glimpsed but not fully grasped. "It all ought to be;—if caused by any apparition of the Divine in me I could bless myself like the Holy mother," she told Sturgis. She meant that she was now beginning to comprehend that her loss of the friendship circle was right and necessary. Having confessed to Sturgis her deep sense of an unfair abandonment by fate, Fuller vowed a new determination to live beyond this crisis. "Oh Caroline, My soul swells with the future. The past I know it not." Her quarrel with Emerson, however, was part of her past, and she admitted to Sturgis that "his call bids me return," and though "I know not how, yet full of tender renunciation, know not how to refuse" (*FL* 2:167). She could not walk away from Emerson completely, but she recognized she must accept a limited and more pragmatic friendship with him.

The most illuminating portrait of their continuing friendship is her journal record of a stay of almost six weeks with the Emerson family and other visitors that began on August 17, 1842. Brought to publication in 1973 by Joel Myerson, this manuscript is "one of the longest and most complete of her extant fragmentary journals,"[11] and covers a period in which Ralph Waldo and Lidian Emerson continued to grieve over the death of their son Waldo the previous January. Fuller's account of the stay included scenes of the troubled Emerson marriage in which Lidian, who was also fighting illness at the time, "burst into tears, at the sight of me," and was again driven to tears another day at the dinner table. "The family were all present, they looked at their plates. Waldo looked on the ground, but soft & serene as ever" (J42 331). This visit seems to have convinced Fuller that despite her continuing admiration for Emerson, "we do not act powerfully on one another" (J42 323). She took several walks and had long conversations with him during this visit, including moments of playfulness in which Fuller "laughed & thought we should certainly never cease to be young" (J42 333). Nevertheless, the intensity of their exchanges had clearly lessened. "Waldo and I have good meetings, though we stop at all our old places. But my expectations are moderate now; it is his beautiful presence that I prize, far more than our intercourse" (J42 326). After a walk on a "golden afternoon," Fuller noted how "we got to talking, as we almost always do, on Man and Woman, and Marriage." Recounting the discussion, she provided this perceptive summation of Emerson's concept of friendship, the issue long disputed between them:

> W. took his usual ground. Love is only phenomenal, a contrivance of nature, in her circular motion. Man, in proportion as he is completely unfolded is man and woman by turns. The soul knows nothing of marriage, in the sense of a permanent union between two personal existences. The soul is married to each new thought as it enters into it. If this thought puts on the form of man or woman[,] if it last you seventy years, what then? There is but one love, that of the Soul of all Souls, let it put on what cunning disguises it will, still at last you find yourself lonely,— *the Soul*. (J42 330)

The apparent despondency of Emerson's views may have been the product of his grief. He was writing "Experience" at this time, an essay that wrestles with loneliness and disconnection. He had also begun the poem "Threnody," a eulogy for his lost son. Yet Fuller called this "his usual ground," making it clear that a significant change of his attitude was unlikely. Fuller continued, however, to strengthen her belief that she had not exhausted her capacity for change and growth. Despite her stinging loss, she was coming to know herself now as "manifold," diverse, heterogeneous, cosmopolitan. She had suffered her own pain and realized her capacity to see, and to sympathize with, the pain of others.

"Arise! Let us go forth!"

The most important role in Fuller's self-remaking was taking charge of *The Dial* in 1840 as the public voice of transcendentalism. The work of Hedge, Ripley, and others had appeared in the Unitarian *Christian Examiner*, a journal focused primarily on theology. Emerson had long pondered establishing a journal, and after Clarke began the *Western Messenger* in distant

Louisville, the idea gained more momentum when the Transcendental Club was founded in 1836. But who could launch and edit such an enterprise? Hedge, Fuller's friend and mentor from her Cambridge days, was the major advocate for a journal, but his pulpit duties in Maine eliminated him from active organization or editorial duties. With Hedge out of the picture, Emerson consulted with Fuller about the journal's fate.[12] Fuller's 1839 translation of Eckermann's *Conversations with Goethe* had recently garnered great respect from both Emerson and Ripley, and it was becoming clear that interest in literature and poetry was growing among the transcendentalists. Fuller had built her intellectual identity on her mastery of modern German literature, keeping a distance from the theological issues that first defined the movement. As she had written to Hedge in 1835, when a magazine for the new views was first being discussed, she would gladly contribute to the work, but, she warned, "I fear I am merely 'Germanico,' and not 'transcendental'" (*FL* 1:226). The need for *The Dial*, and the plan that the editor would be paid for the work, seemed a strong opportunity. She leapt at the chance. As we consider it now, the *Dial*'s historical significance rests in the literary and intellectual openings that it offered Fuller.

During their earlier discussions, the transcendentalists seem to have been strongly supportive of a magazine, but when Fuller began assembling the first issue, she was by no means deluged with contributions. Ripley was buried in editing the immense *Specimens of Foreign Standard Literature*. Hedge had taken the pulpit of a conservative church in Maine and was troubled by the possibility of being condemned as a transcendentalist radical. Even William Henry Channing, who would become Fuller's close friend, initially begged off. With Fuller's patience and persistence, and her ability to negotiate, cajole, and plead, all three of these influential figures eventually contributed to the first or second issue of *The Dial*. More importantly, Fuller brought Samuel Ward and Caroline Sturgis into the first issues.[13] The *Dial* that Fuller assembled was worlds apart from the *Christian Examiner*. Its first issue had more poetry than theology, and its range of genres was more notable than its radical ideas. Poetry was the best-represented literary form, but the issue also included an array of other writings: book reviews by Ripley and William Dexter Wilson, journal passages from Emerson's late brother Charles, essays by Henry David Thoreau and John Sullivan Dwight, and a sermonic essay by Theodore Parker. The first installment of "Ernest the Seeker," Channing's didactic fictional narrative, also appeared, a work that did not augur a novelist's career for him. Ridiculed, and still quaintly representative of transcendental excess, were the fourteen pages of Amos Bronson Alcott's woolly "Orphic Sayings." Alcott had apparently taken a cue from James Freeman Clarke's 1836 translation of a group of Goethe's poems under the title "Orphic Sayings" for the *Western Messenger*. His efforts to articulate the ineffable, however, have baffled most readers, then and now.[14]

With *The Dial* her responsibility, Fuller herself began to experiment in various literary forms, sometimes using her compositions to express her emotional distress. Her entry into fiction early in 1841, a step whose significance was largely neglected until the late twentieth century, was one of her boldest and most original decisions. The idea first arose during a visit from Dr. William Eustis, a somewhat eccentric friend of the Fuller family. He lived reclusively and held a particular interest in plants. Knowing him to be "wearisome" (*FL* 2:164), Fuller found that Eustis's discourse on flowers instead fascinated her. "Then the flowers! I liked to hear him, for he recorded all their pretty ways,—not like a botanist, but a lover." She described "his interview with the Magnolia of Lake Pontchartrain" as "most romantic," and he also added a summary of "what he said of the Yuca," another exotic flowering plant (*FL* 2:165). Fuller quickly realized the mythic and symbolic dimensions of Eustis's discussion of flowers. "Might this not be made into a true poem, if written out merely as history of the plant, and no observer introduced?" she thought. "How finely it harmonizes with all legends of Isis, Diana, &c!" (*FL* 2:166). She published "The Magnolia of Lake Pontchartrain" in *The Dial*'s second issue. Megan Marshall terms this story "a radical shift," suggesting that Fuller was now freeing herself from a perspective "in which creative artists are all men" (Marshall 161). This change would be further confirmed a year later in "Yuca Filamentosa," a story that reflected the "Magnolia" fable's moonlit, deeply feminine atmosphere. Both stories center on flowers that are exemplars of their human chroniclers. They were, for Fuller, reflections of her own experience.

"The Magnolia of Lake Pontchartrain" is an extended conversation between a human narrator and a magnolia blossom. The intense fragrance of a flower captures the narrator along the shore of Lake Pontchartrain as he stops to listen to the magnolia's sorrowful tale. Capper describes the Germanic roots of the stories, noting both "Novalis's flower symbolism" and the German romantics' literary fairy tales (Capper 2:45). Jeffrey Steele also emphasizes their mythological basis, observing that Fuller searched for "transcendent images of divine womanhood."[15] Of particular importance is Dorri Beam's observation that Fuller used the popular flower language of her period to advance her "project of rethinking 'woman' in the nineteenth century."[16] Fuller complicated, and deepened, the impact of the tale by embodying herself in each partner of the dialogue. The Rider, Steele explains, "seems to switch gender as 'he' both represents a vision of Emerson and depicts facets of Fuller's own personality" (Steele 74). Not only do we see her as the roving and intensely curious narrator who interviews the blossom, but also she stands as the blossom itself.

It is important to understand that Fuller structured "The Magnolia" as a mirrored interchange between the narrator and the flower. The magnolia reveals herself to a sympathetic companion, who had herself struggled with the same anxieties as the flower. The sense of shared experience between them is essential. The magnolia learns that the narrator had "through privation, been initiated to the secret of peace." In her suffering she "was driven back upon the centre of [her] being, and there found all being" (EMF 47). Perhaps the most intriguing element of the story for a modern reader is Fuller's use of supernatural figures such as the articulate magnolia blossom and "the queen and guardian of the flowers." The queen is "a being of another order from thee," the flower tells her, and "a goddess, larger and statelier of proportion, an angel,—like still, only with an added power." This form of mystical fable allowed Fuller to represent her experience as beyond the conventional boundaries of thought and gender. As the magnolia explains, "Man never creates, he only recombines the lines and colors of his own existence; only a deific fancy could evolve from the elements the form that took me home." While "Man" means "human" here, it also evokes "male," and in this case Fuller's magnolia is clearly a female rescued by a female goddess. As if to emphasize the gendered nature of her rebirth, the magnolia declares that her rescue was the result of feminine power, that of the divine goddess. "Secret, radiant, profound ever, and never to be known, was she; many forms indicate and none declare her. Like all such beings she was feminine. All the secret powers are 'Mothers.' There is but one paternal power" (*EMF* 48). Fuller thus employed supernatural events, reported by a fictional female narrator, to express and explain her personal crisis through that of another woman.

The most important feature of the "Magnolia" narrative is the portrayal of the orange tree's transformation, which appears to be an act of magic performed by the queen of the flowers. Fuller crafted the details of this shift of identities carefully, making clear that her own plight is reflected in that of the magnolia. She adeptly utilized this nineteenth-century female discourse to dissolve the boundary between the human and the natural, and between the natural and the spiritual. As Beam recognizes, the effectiveness of Fuller's craft was in her "sense of an alternative ontology," a capacity to create "a mode of pleasure and way of being that is not rooted in gendered anatomy" (Beam 6). Using well-known traditions of flower language and more recent forms of mesmeric and spiritualist mysticism, Fuller found a means to express the human by way of the transhuman, using imagined modes of experiential capability to confront the gendered confinement that women encountered. In voicing her own pain through the "spirit" (*EMF* 46) of a blossom, Fuller took into herself the natural qualities of a plant and then infused the plant with a trans-material identity—with a soul. She gave this "natural" blossom a history, insisting that her experience is not fixed but open. It is open, as we find, to tragedy, but also to a new and radically different life. In her striving to be a useful, fruitful plant, the orange has led a completely other-directed life and lost her essential self. In so doing, she has also lost her connection to the larger supporting web of nature.

Fuller's depiction of the abandoned flower resonated strongly with her own sense of rejection and loss. In a close reading, the restorative aspects of the narrative are unmistakable. "The inaccessible sun looked at me with the same ray as on all others; my endless profusion could not bribe him to one smile sacred to me alone. The mysterious wind passed me by to tell its secret to the solemn pine. And the nightingale sang to the rose, rather than me, though she was often silent, and buried herself yearly in the dark earth." The flower's lament captures the sense of exhaustion and abuse that Fuller dramatized in this narrative. "I had no mine or thine, I belonged to all, I could never rest, I was never at one" (*EMF* 47). Abandoned by both humanity and nature, the depleted orange tree is touched by a frigid breeze, "a cold white beam from those stranger worlds," and is physically killed by the frost. Separated from its leaves and branches, the disembodied spirit of the tree speaks of feeling "a mystic shudder of pale joy" that "separated me wholly from my former abode." The tree's bodily death, however, is not an ultimate or permanent death but a joyful release of its essence. It is at this point that the spirit of the tree, taken into protection by another mystical presence, "the queen and guardian of the flowers," is released to the new life of the magnolia (*EMF* 48).

The released spirit of the orange tree goes to its new life with this cautionary advice from its queen: "Take a step inward, forget a voice, lose a power; no longer a bounteous sovereign, become a vestal priestess and bide thy time in the Magnolia" (*EMF* 49). Notice that the advice is for gradual change—"take *a* step," "forget *a* voice"—not for a sudden and complete change of identity. She is warned against "the vehemence of [her] desire," which "at once promises and forbids its gratification" (*EMF* 49). The spirit of the orange blossom is not immediately healed and made into a magnolia but becomes a being who must willfully begin healing and re-forming itself by deliberate steps. The spirit in the magnolia that had attracted the narrator thus remains that of an orange blossom. As the flower explained earlier, "my root is the same" although "in my family I have no sister of the heart" (*EMF* 46). She is a spirit who has made an inward turn, a retreat from public life and servitude to others, to devote herself more completely to self-understanding. The tree must protect itself from the demands of others; she must resist the impulse to please others. She must sing in isolation to reclaim her identity.

The second of Fuller's flower stories, "Yuca Filamentosa," carries a new mood of poise and serenity, describing the nocturnal blossoming of two rarely flowering yucca plants. This event takes place under the full light of the moon, an illustration of the vitality of a lunar feminine principle. The events of the moonlight blossoming are related by a narrator who reverently observes them as a sacred ceremony, an enactment of "the fulfillment of nobleness" (*EMF* 44) that keys "The Magnolia of Lake Pontchartrain." The narrator reveals herself as a searcher for harmony and accord in her opening comment, "Often, as I have looked up to the moon, I have marvelled to see how calm she was in her loneliness." Building on the mythical and folkloric traditions that shaped a feminine moon and a masculine sun, Fuller's narrator asks for "some living hieroglyphic to indicate that class of emotions which the moon calls up" (*EMF* 50). She searches for security in the sign that opens the moon's mystical feminine consciousness to her. She is seeking her female goddess.

The narrator unexpectedly finds herself in the spiritual realm when she notices two barren yucca plants in her garden, the larger of which "was preparing to flower." She watches it "eagerly," fascinated but impatient with its slowly unfolding buds. When the weaker plant also begins to bud, she is greeted by "the slender crescent of the young moon" (*EMF* 51), signifying the lunar power that has vitalized the plants. Continuing to watch during the moon's waxing in the ensuing days, she recognizes that "the one, which had budded first, seemed to be waiting for the other." That intuition is confirmed dramatically when, with the arrival of "the night of the full moon," both plants "burst into flower together" (*EMF* 51). It is not the flowering only but the vital bond between the yucca plants that is of great spiritual importance in this event. It is as if they were interacting in a deliberately harmonious way. The presence of the full moon, creator of the event, further sanctifies the flowers' blossoming in unison, which in itself is an act of worship of the goddess-moon. The narrator describes the ceremony with an aural rather than a visual metaphor, naming it "a night of long-sought melody" (*EMF* 51). Quiet though it may be, it is an orchestrated joy, celebrating both the self-fulfillment signaled by the achievement of each blossom and the greater achievement of their simultaneity and accord.

"Yuca Filamentosa" is Fuller's most deeply spiritual literary work. That spirituality is expressed through harmony, a concept of great significance to her in this moment. The flowers are in harmony with the moon, and with each other, and thereby generate a spectacle of worshipful moonlit celebration. The flowers' cohesive performance, which represents their willed desire to bond through the energy of the moon, carries multiple meanings. Through the moon's dual identities as an elemental and spiritual power, the bonded blossoming plants illustrate the fused mytho-natural laws that govern all experience. Fuller too blossoms under the full moon. "After months of mystical exhilaration, depression, and fable writing," Capper observes, "Fuller seems to have reached some sort of catharsis." Feeling as if she had been visited by angels in her dreams during an early August night in 1841, she appears to have found "some form of the feminine 'self-recognition' and self-acceptance that had heretofore eluded her" (Capper 2:48, 49).

In the year between the publication of "The Magnolia" and "Yuca," Fuller composed a quite different story. The weirdly commanding "Leila," a complex, dreamlike character portrait, defies final and exact description. Capper terms it both "darkly visionary" and "gnarled and obscure" (Capper 2:46), descriptions that suggest the range of emotions that the story generates. Fuller's troubled meditation focused on the mysterious but empowering shadow-self. Steele, whose reading of the story assured its place in the Fuller canon, terms the figure Leila "a profound symbol of transfigured womanhood" (Steele 84). The story's narrative voice is that of an unnamed figure, most likely a sibling, who has known and observed Leila from childhood. All she tells us is that "we grew up together with name and home and parentage" (*EMF* 54). Leila enacts through her alternating rapture and agony the desires held forbidden in the conventional experience of women. Hers is a depiction of the rebuilding of a life after a trauma. The occult dimensions of Leila's performance, and the portrayal of her alternating rapture and agony, suggest that Fuller wrote "Leila" with energy and exploratory creativity but did so under intense emotional pressure. Leila has realized that her extraordinary powers are insufficient to generate a completely transformed earth. "Leila, with wild hair scattered to the wind, bare and often bleeding feet, opiates and divining rods in each over-full hand, walked amid the habitations of mortals as a Genius, visited their consciences as a Demon" (*EMF* 56–57). Fuller portrayed the defeat of a wise and powerful woman, battling for high ideals in an imperfect world. Leila is transformed from a prophetess and savior figure into a tragic witness to the limitations of hope. This change can be read as Fuller's tragic self-analysis.

Fuller's Leila thus stands as a figure of enlightenment and triumphant redemption, but as a witness to human tragedy too. The narrator also follows Leila's pattern of gaining, and then losing, transcendent truth. Leila's loss has been hers as well, and their natures seem forever bonded in this calamity. Fuller created Leila as an inspirational goddess, but she was also intent on writing a fable that would remind her readers that transcendent vision and mythical power are in themselves insufficient guides and supports. She structured her narrative to ensure that the reader understands that a moment's mystical insight does not in itself alter the burdens of human limitations. Even the goddess Leila stands bent and humbled by experience, representing the power of the visionary and in addition its tragic inadequacy. It is only through the strengthening of human bonds that Leila and her narrator can claim hope, and as Fuller's narrative proclaims, "The hour is come for still deeper trust. Arise! Let us go forth!" (*EMF* 58).

"We are not ripe to reconstruct society yet"

While Fuller was filling *The Dial* with mythical and occult fiction, a different form of new energy was also building. In the January 1842 issue Fuller published Elizabeth Palmer Peabody's "Plan of the West Roxbury Community," a discussion of the Brook Farm commune's goals and principles.[17] The Brook Farmers, led by George Ripley, would eventually embrace Fourierism, the political theory that was making a powerful impact on American progressives. Albert Brisbane, with his 1843 volume *Association*—"Associationism" being an attractively named version of the theory—became the leading American voice of Fourierism. Brisbane had studied for several years in Germany and France as a young man and eventually met Charles Fourier in 1832. He was particularly attracted by the pragmatic quality of Fourier's social philosophy and converted to Fourierism when he saw one particular term in Fourier's texts: "attractive industry" (*industrie attrayante*). People were attracted to work, Fourier believed, but were drawn individually to differing ways of effort. By organizing them in harmony with their passions, Fourier argued, labor would become liberating. Such a dream was possible, he preached, through the concept of "association," a reorganization of social institutions through the natural attractions that guided the acts of men and women. "ASSOCIATION is the SOCIAL DESTINY of Man," Brisbane proclaimed. It "is the true and natural system of Society, predestined for him by the Creator, and will, when established upon earth, secure to him that happiness for which he has so long sought in vain."[18]

Fuller's close friend William Henry Channing had become one of the most ardent followers of Associationism among the transcendentalists. The nephew of William Ellery Channing, saint of New England Unitarianism, Channing had followed his uncle into the ministry and found himself unsatisfied with the moderate disposition of Unitarianism. He believed that he could develop a more spiritual form of Associationism, a merger of liberal religiosity and socialist politics able to reform the problematic situation of the time. In 1843 Channing established the Christian Union of Associationists in New York, a church that he hoped would become a vehicle for uniting religion and Associationism into an active force for political change. His statement of the organization's principles referred to the plight of the urban poor, which he had encountered in New York, as a distressing sign of the times. "Masses are crowded into narrow places, foul airs, and situations engendering disease. Society expends in the punishment of criminals, sums, which justly shared, would have insured the virtue of these victims of neglect. All suffer for the common wrong."[19] Condemning the individualist view of transcendentalism, he argued that "God reveals himself more fully" in a collective environment, "where men are bound together in mutual sympathy and respect, in justice, truth and love, in common joy" (CU 7). Channing was frank with Emerson, whom he highly regarded. In 1842 he wrote to him to praise his "Divinity School Address" after recently rereading it. "It says all that can be said from that point of view." This work, however, and "all that I have read of your writings" have "one radical defect, which, like a wound in the bark, wilts and blights the leaf and bloom and fruit of your faith." The defect is individualism. "You deny the Human Race. You stand, or rather seek to stand, a complete Adam. But you cannot do it."[20] Channing's direct assault on Emerson's "radical defect" provides a glimpse of his fervor in his crusade for Associationism.

Launching the Christian Union was his boldest attempt at putting the principle of "mutual sympathy" to work as a tool of reform. While guiding the Christian Union, Channing also threw much of his torrid energy into *The Present*, a reform journal that gave him a platform in the reform discourse of the early 1840s. He opened it with a detailed essay titled "Social Reorganization," which offered his own version of the Fourierist doctrine that restructuring human labor would release enormously constructive interaction among men and women. "There is strife in trade, not merely between empires, but in country and cities, of class with class and man with man, in endless competition."[21] This furious antagonism weakens society and destroys the intuitive mutual sympathies that are the hope of true community. "By chains or cunning, by the lash or legal provisions, by the whip or wages, man makes his brother a slave." Channing's startling equation of commerce and slavery was a demand for the redefinition of labor itself, the place from which Fourier had launched his utopian vision of reform. As Channing wrote: "Labor is, not a curse, but a privilege, an honor, and its own reward. Work is imitation of God's creative power" (*Present* 42). Channing, like Brisbane, followed Fourier's theory that the innate drive to work, in its widest sense, would counter the oppression and misery of modern life if a just organization of the production of goods could be realized.

Fuller was also feeling an urge for reformism. As she wrote to Channing in 1840: "My dear friend, you speak of your sense of 'unemployed force.'—I feel the same. I never, never in life have had the happy feeling of really ever doing any thing." The literary work she had done as a critic and translator seemed to her "semblances of actions" that might perhaps give some aid to others. "But Oh! really to feel the glow of action, without its weariness, what heaven it must be!" (*FL* 2:126). Her exchange of letters with Channing in the early 1840s shows a sense of concerned obligation impeded by vocational uncertainty. She believed that her skills were needed but found difficulty in productively locating herself. There was, however, more literary than political discussion in Fuller's letters to Channing. Drawn by his sharp recognition of injustice and his compassion for the poor and oppressed, she could not fully accept the utopian optimism of his politics. "We are not ripe to reconstruct society yet," she told him frankly (FL 2:194). Fuller visited Brook Farm and surely wished it well but doubted its success. In an 1841 letter that captured her reluctant skepticism, she described seeing George Ripley go "out to his farm yesterday, full of cheer, as one who doeth a deed with sincere good will. He has shown a steadfastness and earnestness of purpose most grateful to behold. I do not know what their scheme will ripen to; at present it does not deeply engage my hopes" (FL 2:205).

"The Great Lawsuit"

The Dial had been successful in many ways under Fuller's editorial guidance, but it had not been profitable. In the spring of 1842, weak subscription sales and the bankruptcy of its publisher made it clear that Fuller would not be paid for her work and that the journal would completely crash. After much discussion, Emerson agreed to take over as editor, giving *The Dial* two more years of production. While Fuller was sad to leave her editorial role, it was beneficial for her. With those duties behind her, she could focus on the concern developing in her for a decade or more: the rights of women. Her response was quick. "The Great Lawsuit. Man *versus* Men. Woman *versus* Women" was published in *The Dial* a year later. As Marshall writes, it "would prove to be *The Dial*'s most enduring contribution to American thought" (Marshall 210). Fuller was more certain that modern women now must claim the life and the society that they deserved. The "Lawsuit" that she laid out was "Great" because it called for two major social changes, one for men and one for women. Fuller's somewhat complex subtitle, "Man *versus* Men. Woman *versus* Women," suggested that each sex must be called upon to recognize and realize its moral responsibilities.[22]

Men must strive to represent "Man" at its best and fullest capacity, and Women too must bring themselves to become the finest examples of "Woman." The irony of her title, as Phyllis Cole has written, was that the term "Lawsuit" had "named a means of public remediation to which," at this time, "women had no access." As the daughter of a prominent attorney, Fuller surely understood that her suit could only be adjudicated by "the higher law of divine nature," the ultimate standard of justice.[23] The irony of her title thus becomes the proof of her complaint. The task of Fuller's essay was not to demonstrate how to change the existing laws but to bring women and men to embrace an understanding of why those laws must be changed. Modern readers, for the most part, cannot fully realize how radical Fuller's propositions were when she published them. Her ideas would, if enacted, have upended life as it was lived in the 1840s.

Fuller explained that the effort to bring "Man" and "Woman" to a higher stage of fulfillment was not a new phenomenon but a project that "has now been carried through many ages, with various results." It had at last discovered a "foundation" (GL 1), an "inheritance" that, if realized, promised a "future Eden" (GL 3). Her prophetic assurance was grounded in a principle that was stressed throughout the essay: the elevation of women is also the elevation of men. The full recognition of the capability and worth of women was the next step of human evolution, inevitable, Fuller believed, because female and male are manifestations of the same "soul," a term that expressed both the sacred self of everyone and the shared nature of all selves. "Whatever the soul knows how to seek, it must attain. Knock, and it shall be opened; seek, and ye shall find" (GL 4). Fuller believed that the freeing of women was a moral, even religious responsibility, which could be expressed politically as the achievement of women's liberty. This was the same quest that had, in recent human history, fueled the democratic struggles against monarchical, racial, and colonialist oppression. "A new manifestation is at hand, a new hour in the day of man," she wrote (GL 5). It would be a mankind that encompassed two equal sexes. This democratic impulse would continue through a deeper comprehension of women's rights. "As the principle of liberty is better understood and more nobly interpreted, a broader protest is made in behalf of woman" (GL 7). It was on this basis that Fuller emphasized "the changes demanded by the champions of woman," as the actual new world that was now arriving. "We would have every arbitrary barrier thrown down. We would have every path laid open to woman as freely as to man" (GL 14). The opportunities that these alterations would provide—notably, the opening of doors and unlocking of chains—would perhaps generate a "slight temporary fermentation" but would also allow "the Divine" to "ascend into nature to a height unknown in the history of past ages" and ultimately bring "ravishing harmony" (GL 14).

Fuller's vision of the new liberty for women was near-apocalyptic, and most impressively, it exposed the enormous release of positive and productive energy that remained locked away under patriarchy.[24] Women's protests could not be answered solely by granting women new status in the social and economic worlds. The new world Fuller envisioned would arrive only "when inward and outward freedom for woman, as much as for man, shall be acknowledged as a right, not yielded as a concession" (GL 14). Fuller connected the women's movement to the rising antislavery movement and expounded the sacredness of each soul as the essential basis of truth. Melding democratic rights with devoutly sanctified values, she presented the women's movement as both egalitarian and hallowed, a crusade for justice and for moral principle. "As the friend of the negro assumes that one man cannot, by right, hold another in bondage, so should the friend of woman assume that man cannot, by right, lay even well-meant restrictions on woman. If the negro be a soul, if the woman be a soul, appareled in flesh, to one master only are they accountable." Insisting on the basic truth, she wrote that "there is but one law for all souls, and, if there is to be an interpreter of it, he comes not as man, or son of man, but as Son of God" (GL 14). This proclamation marked one of the essay's peaks, providing a trenchant answer to resistance toward women's rights and establishing the fundamental principle of the sacred soul as the support for the coming social transformation.

It is here that Fuller introduced her model of the nineteenth-century woman, Miranda, through a conversational sketch, framed as an interview with an exceptional, almost ideal figure, who had "taken a course of her own, and no man had stood in her way" (GL 15). She is also a self-portrait and a seeming repudiation of her earlier "Autobiographical Romance." Fuller had written that scathing account of her father's punishing educational practices perhaps as late as October 1841 (Capper 2:47–48), not that distant from the spring of 1843, when she wrote "The Great Lawsuit." The Miranda we meet there appears to be the fortunate product of the same strict treatment. Miranda was her father's "eldest child and came to him at an age when he needed a companion. From the time she could speak and go alone, he addressed her not as a plaything, but as a living mind." As a result, she became "a child of the spirit," living "in the world of mind" with "a dignified sense of self-dependence" (GL 15). This Miranda is not the damaged child we saw in the "Autobiographical Romance." Fuller reminds us that neither text should be read as her entire biographical truth. "The Great Lawsuit" does suggest, however, that Fuller had made a strong recovery from her breakdown over the loss of Ward and Barker and her deep disappointment with Emerson. Despite her father's mistreatment, she had come to see his gift to her: a "world of mind" and a "sense of self-dependence." The world, as she said of Miranda, "was free to her, and she lived freely in it" (GL 15). Perhaps the clearest evidence of Fuller's restored strength was her decision to write "The Great Lawsuit." It required engagement in a hotly controversial public debate, extensive reading, and, most importantly, the confidence that she could effectively challenge deeply ingrained social injustice.

Near the end of her comments, Miranda makes one observation that casts a shadow over the future of the women's movement. "But early," she warns, "I perceived that men never, in any extreme of despair, wished to be women. Where they admired any woman they were inclined to speak of her as above her sex." In Miranda's voice, Fuller described "a rooted skepticism, which for ages has been fastening on the heart, and which only an age of miracles could eradicate" (GL 16). Miranda's candid reproach of men's embedded conceit took "The Great Lawsuit" into controversial discussions that supported the male sense of ownership or superiority. Marriage and its confined female domestic sphere were central to this issue, and though yet unmarried, Fuller described that institution knowingly. She argued that marriage had done little to recognize or establish the fulfillment of women's capabilities. Marriage had failed to allow women "the freedom, the religious, the intelligent freedom of the universe" (GL 23). It had instead been the greatest barrier to women. Fuller systematically described the forms of marriage, rising from the humdrum "household partnership" of "mutual esteem, mutual dependence," to the distasteful "mutual idolatry" in which the partners "weaken and narrow one another" (GL 28). She observed, however, "an onward tendency" in the modern marriages of "intellectual companionship" (GL 30), noting Mary Wollstonecraft and George Sand as examples, even though they faced public scorn. Fuller defined the highest and truest form of marriage as "religious," a dedication to a "pilgrimage towards a common shrine," which unified the partners in such a way that they could continually develop in all understanding and practice. This marriage was not an exclusion of the world, but included "home sympathies, and household wisdom," and also a companionship of thought that can nurture "more glorious prospects that open as we advance" (GL 32).

The idea of continuing advancement for individuals and society sustained Fuller's vision of the liberation of women. The roots of this vision were in the concept of the "soul," which could be thought of as the fundamental creative energy, alive in the cosmos and in each living individual. The soul was, for both Fuller and Emerson, the expression of the monistic character of the universe. The cosmos, even in its vastness and variety, was a single element. As Emerson poetically phrased it: "We live in succession, in division, in parts, in particles. Meantime within man is the soul of the whole; the wise silence; the universal beauty, to which every part and particle is equally related; the eternal ONE" (CW 2:160). It was this belief in the all-encompassing soul that gave Fuller the language for the most striking and memorable passages in "The Great Lawsuit." The "soul" presented a proto-theory of gender that equalized women and men while emphasizing women's distinct strengths. Fuller was clearly aware of "The Over-Soul" (1841), Emerson's articulation of this concept, and she also looked to Novalis in working out a theo-philosophical outlook that averted the mind-matter dichotomy.[25] For Fuller and Emerson, reality was "one," but a "one" that was in perpetual process. "There is no other world," as Emerson wrote. "Here or nowhere is the whole fact; all the Universe over, there is but one thing,—this old double, Creature-creator, mind-matter, right-wrong"

(*JMN* 8:182–83). While Fuller continued, on occasion, to use conventional religious terminology, she turned to this monistic language of the soul in "The Great Lawsuit" in order to communicate a sense of onward advancing development for women. It expressed a metamorphic energy that was both immanent in the self and manifest in the events of the world.

This discourse was congruent with the magnetic or mesmeric forces in which she had taken such interest. These energies were, she felt, gestures of the progressing soul still to be investigated and interpreted. "The electrical, the magnetic element in woman has not been fairly developed at any period," she contended. "Everything might be expected from it; she has far more of it than man" (GL 38). Fuller's interest in the availability of unrecognized, unexplored forms of perception was central to her broader emphasis on the educational growth of women. She referred to Justinus Kerner's *Seeress of Prevorst*, a book she soon analyzed in detail in *Summer on the Lakes*, as an example of a modern woman infused with magnetic awareness.[26] Even though the "Seeress" was disdained, she was also, wrote Fuller, through Kerner's work, "the first, or the best observed subject of magnetism in our times" (GL 38). For Fuller the "magnetic" was not an otherworldly séance but a rarely encountered form of deeper perception that could be more widely opened to women. Fuller was driven by the belief that she was living in an era of women's awakening, in which a newly released female energy was beginning to transform human culture. "In so far as soul is in her completely developed, all soul is the same; but as far as it is modified in her as woman, it flows, it breathes, it sings, rather than deposits soil, or finishes work," she declared. "That which is especially feminine flushes in blossom the face of the earth, and pervades like air and water all this seeming solid globe, daily renewing and purifying its life" (GL 43). Fuller's emphasis on a female principle or essence enabled her to characterize the unmerited suppression of one form of humanity. She added one important point. "Femality," she insisted, "is no more the order of nature that it should be incarnated pure in any form, than that the masculine should exist unmingled with it in any form" (GL 43). Men and women were both "masculine" and "feminine."

Fuller had come to recognize these truths through her friendship circle. "I loved Anna [Barker] for a time I think with as much passion as I was then strong enough to feel," she wrote in an absorbing 1842 journal entry. "Her face was always gleaming before me, her voice was echoing in my ear, all poetic thoughts clustered round the dear image." Barker's friendship, she wrote, had been a deepening influence on her understanding of the nature of friendship. "This love was a key that unlocked for me many a treasure which I still possess, it was the carbuncle (emblematic gem) which cast light into many of the darkest caverns of human nature." Fuller described her relationship not simply as an admiration of Barker but as a mutual love that overcame the differences in temperament between them. "She loved me too, though not so much, because her nature was 'less high, less grave, less large, less deep' but she loved more tenderly, less passionately." Beyond her beauty, Barker had a warmth and empathy made for friendship. Unlike the others in this group, she did not seem to have high literary or artistic ambitions, though she greatly admired Fuller. Barker's charm, tenderness, and spirituality enthralled Fuller, who had come to regard her as the model of the feminine character. "It is so true that a woman may be in love with a woman, and a man with a man, Fuller wrote.[27]

Fuller's articulation of the dualism within the monistic soul, the two sexes with one encompassing identity, is one of the most notable passages in "The Great Lawsuit." "Male and female represent the two sides of the great radical dualism. But, in fact, they are perpetually passing into one another. Fluid hardens to solid, solid rushes to fluid. There is no wholly masculine man, no purely feminine women" (GL 43). The term "radical" evokes the essential and deep-rooted character of this dualism, a force that is enduring. But "radical" in a more modern sense evoked that which is extreme, uncompromising, and disputed, implying the division of the sexes. Yet this division is perpetually melting and flowing, altering and converting itself, never settled. Fuller speaks here not only of the flowing natures of women and men but also of a creation that is always changing. This continuing rush, as she calls it, explains why, in human character and development, "nature provides exceptions to every rule" (GL 43). The classifications feminine and masculine are never absolute or permanent, and their attributes are found among all. From this perspective, Fuller appealed for a unified effort of all women and men to open the social pathways that would result in the free development of all individuals. "Let us be wise and not impede the soul. Let her work as she will. Let us have one creative energy, one incessant revelation. Let it take what form it will, and let us not bind it by the past to man or woman, black or white" (GL 44).

CHAPTER 4
Vital Energy

"The Hatred Felt by the White Man"

Soon after the completion of "The Great Lawsuit," James Freeman Clarke and his sister Sarah Ann Clarke offered Fuller an opportunity to travel with them on an extensive tour of the American frontier. Fuller welcomed it as a needed rest and an intriguing chance to see the burgeoning settlements and the renowned western landscape. She went, however, with some concern. "I come to the West prepared for the distaste I must experience at its mushroom growth. I know that, where 'go ahead' is the only motto, the village cannot grow into gentle proportions that successive lives, and the gradations of experience involuntarily give." Comparing the American move west to a "warlike invasion," she prepared to encounter the inevitable "rudeness of conquest" awaiting her. "I have come prepared to see all this, to dislike it, but not with stupid narrowness to distrust or defame." She hoped to see "a new order, a new poetry" that would "be evoked from this chaos" (*EMF* 86). Her essay had brought out the need for reformation on behalf of women's rights. Fuller's journey was, in this sense, a testing of America. Through the lens of women's subjugation, she would be able to observe the needs and accomplishments on the frontier. She was exhausted by her work at *The Dial*, but the West brought a new energy. That energy would lead to her first book.

She kept a journal during the trip and wrote descriptive letters to several friends, but as Susan Belasco notes, the actual composition of *Summer on the Lakes* occurred, with some difficulties, after her return. The book began to come together in the late fall of 1843, when she immersed herself in the Harvard library's collection of travel books, focusing on works "that dealt with exploration of the Indian territories."[1] Fuller was endeavoring to come to terms with the American exploitation of the Native people of the West. While reflections of "The Great Lawsuit" appeared throughout this new work, Fuller encountered friction between her vision of women's emancipation and the despairing circumstances of the dispersed Native tribes. "The Great Lawsuit" had been more than a protest against the mistreatment of women. Much of its impact was generated by its resoundingly positive trust in women and their capacities. Fuller wrote with the confidence that women not only should but also would take their rightful places and help construct a better society. "The world at large is readier to let woman learn and manifest the capacities of her nature than it ever was before" (GL 38), she proclaimed, explaining that modern American women now had "time to think, and no traditions to chain them, and few conventionalities compared with what must be met in other nations" (GL 39). The circumstances that had impeded women from their full development were now dissipating, opening new lives for women and new energy and creativity for their communities. Exciting though these advances were, Fuller would learn on her travels how distant they seemed from the frontier.

The grim condition of the Native peoples and the motives that had forced such conditions on them became a troubling concern. Early in the book Fuller described the impact of one of the best-known natural wonders, Niagara Falls, saying that her first views of it yielded "a quiet satisfaction" (*EMF* 72). Oddly, however, as her familiarity with the falls grew, a disturbing sense of dread began to accompany her amazement. "The perpetual trampling of the waters seized my senses," she wrote. "I felt that no other sound, however near, could be heard, and would start and look behind me for a foe." It was as if she had been somehow enclosed by the perpetual din, frozen into a sense of helplessness by the sheer power of the relentless waters. When approaching the falls, she began to see "images, such as never haunted" her mind before: "naked savages stealing behind me with uplifted tomahawks" (*EMF* 72). Her fear suggested a fate that defined the American effort to subdue the continent's Indigenous peoples. Fuller described the falls as an elemental threat. Humans cannot escape or overcome this natural power. Her visceral fear of the falls and her link of the falls to the "savage" were the product of the violent exploitation in the European migration into North America.

Fuller's sense of fear, pity, and deep curiosity established a frame for a more penetrating consideration of the Chippewa and Ottawa tribes on Mackinaw Island. Some two thousand people had encamped by the lake to receive an annual government payment. This gathering gave Fuller an opportunity to observe and interact with the campers in a somewhat festive atmosphere. "I liked very much to walk or sit among them," she wrote, and "with the women I held much communication by signs" (*EMF* 175). As she continued her observation, however, it became clear to her that despite their "decorum and delicacy," the Native women "occupy a lower place than the women among the nations of European civilization." She noted "the habits of drudgery expressed in their form and gesture, the soft and wild but melancholy expression of their eye," indications of the "anguish and weariness" of their lives. She regarded these women with sympathy and concern and saw them as signs that they were denied "their share of the human inheritance" (*EMF* 178). With the fate of women much on her mind, these beleaguered women made a strong impact on her. The cultural traditions and legal boundaries that stood as barriers to American women seemed to be amplified by her encounters with the Native women, because they opened the question of the permanence of women's oppression. Were these women signs that all women would inevitably be denied their due share of human knowledge and self-expression?[2]

Fuller was dismayed by the state of utter dependence that these women seemed to face. They recognized the complete victimization of their husbands and children in the American West. She was stunned by the searing American hatred and contempt for the Native Americans that she discovered, even in the relatively calm areas that she visited. While she knew of "the hatred felt by the white man to the Indian," she wrote, she was utterly dismayed by the "disgust," even "loathing" expressed by the white women, who ignored the Indians' "claims" and "sorrows" with "abhorrence of their dirt, their tawny skins, and the vices the whites had taught them." This bigotry seemed open and abundant in her observations, pushing her to a sizzling denunciation of the American pillaging of the Native peoples and their culture. "Our people and our government have sinned alike against the first-born of the soil," she charged, committing abuses under the name of "holy power." This was a masking of evil that shamed both Christianity and civilization. "Yes! Slave-drivers and Indian traders are called Christians, and the Indian is to be deemed less like the Son of Mary than they!" Fuller snarled. "Wonderful is the deceit of man's heart" (*EMF* 180–81).

As Fuller considered the impact of the displacement of the tribes, the issue of the survival of the Native American pressed upon her. For the Indians, she believed, "amalgamation would afford the only true and profound means of civilization." But this idea had begun to seem impossible, given the racial hatred she had observed. The assimilation of Native Americans might save them and ultimately lead them to civil lives, but after seeing the West, she could not envision a path opening toward this end. "But nature seems, like all else, to declare, that this race is fated to perish," she conceded (*EMF* 188). "I have no hope of liberalizing the missionary, of humanizing the sharks of trade, of infusing the conscientious drop into the flinty bosom of policy, of saving the Indian from immediate degradation and speedy death" (*EMF* 189). The same social forces that accounted for the destruction of Native American cultures also stood as barriers to women's rights. The struggle for the advancement of women was a battle against the same subjugation, one that hinged on the recognition of the sacred selfhood of all women and their right to the power of decision-making in the private and public realm.

"The desolation of solitude"

Although nineteenth-century travel narratives were by custom open to a casual, even rambling compositional technique, Fuller's *Summer on the Lakes* has seemed to many readers annoyingly disjointed. Perry Miller, whose studies of the transcendentalists in the 1950s remain invaluable, was one of the more severe critics of Fuller's account. "Reports on scenes alternate with random associations or with insertions of brazenly extraneous matter," he grumbled, and this resulted in confusion over "the real theme of the narrative—the trip itself."³ It was not until the flood of revisionist Fuller scholarship in the 1970s and 1980s that it became clear that *Summer on the Lakes* was not meant to be a picturesque narrative of the frontier but rather offered a deeper feminist understanding of the connection between a subjugation based on sex and a subjugation based on race. The "brazenly extraneous matter" in *Summer on the Lakes* that Miller condemned consisted primarily of Fuller's story "Mariana" and her discussion of *Die Seherin von Prevorst*, the biography of a German clairvoyant, Frederica Hauffe.⁴ Both of these works focused on the tragic life of a woman with extraordinary capabilities.⁵

"Mariana" is a fictional story with deep autobiographical roots. It traces the experience of a creative, intelligent, but nonconformist student in a girls' boarding school, one like Miss Preston's School in Groton, Massachusetts, which Fuller had attended at age fourteen (Capper 1:82). The story begins with the narrator's startled reaction to the saddening news of the death of Mariana, a remarkable figure she knew in boarding school. "Mariana, so full of life, was dead. That form, the richest in energy and coloring of any I had ever seen, had faded from the earth." What follows is the story of a woman whose remarkable energy and creativity could not find a satisfying and productive course. The narrator tells of coming to know Mariana at their school and worshipping her as a strikingly captivating woman. "She was always new, always surprising, and for a time, charming" (*EMF* 118). She became an outcast, however, who "could never be depended on to join" her schoolmates in their activities. She had "a vein of haughty caprice in her character" and "a love of solitude" (*EMF* 119). This made her, in a school full of girls seeking acceptance from their peers, an outsider. Mariana found her path of self-expression in the "private theatricals" that she organized and directed, and in which she took "the principal parts, as a matter of course" (*EMF* 119–20). She even chose to wear her theatrical makeup during the school day, as if the play continued endlessly. Mocked by her fellow students, she "was quite unprepared to find herself in the midst of a world which despised her" (*EMF* 121).

Fuller's description of Mariana's consequent fall into darkness is Hawthornean in its portrayal of the self-loathing that a damaged soul can generate. Mariana turns to her theatrical talents as a tool of vengeance against her antagonists, pretending to care for them while planting "the seeds of dissension" among them (*EMF* 122). When a group of girls discover that Mariana has plotted against them, her acts are publicly revealed to the entire school. This exposure more than embarrasses her. "I will not, cannot live," she thinks. "The main-spring of [her] life is broken" (*EMF* 124). While Mariana does continue to live, she loses the self-possession and magnetic force that made her so singular. Her "fiery life," Fuller wrote, has "fallen from flame to coal" (*EMF* 125). Mariana's tragic destruction may at first seem a tale of good and evil, but Fuller's emphasis is the loss of Mariana's burning energy.

Fuller's still seething sense of double rejection in the marriage of Ward and Barker is encapsulated in this episode of Mariana's disgrace. We cannot, however, understand this event as mere self-portrayal. Though still riddled with self-pity, Fuller had begun to learn how to transform her emotional pain into social critique, turning her missteps and rejections into a form of guidance for women. The Mariana who emerges from her classmates' antipathy becomes at first calculatingly vengeful but then eventually pitifully dependent. Almost cruelly, in the story's second part, Fuller takes her character through another heartrending experience: marriage. "Mariana" is in this sense two stories—that of the gifted girl who will not conform and that of the independent woman who finds marriage an imprisonment. Fuller had given much thought to the institution of marriage in one of the key sections of "The Great Lawsuit." She describes Mariana's marriage, however, as the shattering misfortune of devoting oneself to an unreceptive partner. Having returned from her New England school to her native South, Mariana is introduced to the attractive Sylvain. "Mariana no sooner met him than she loved, and her love, lovely as she was, soon excited his." Their marriage before long becomes a suffocating dead end. Fuller describes Mariana's intellectual and magnetic energy uselessly proffered to Sylvain, a man of both ability and kindness, but incapable of recognizing or responding to the attributes that give Mariana her extraordinary personality. "Thoughts he had none, and little delicacy of sentiment," Fuller writes. "Deeply in love," and holding tightly to the hope that she can eventually achieve "further communion" with her husband, Mariana begins to feel "the desolation of solitude, and a repression of her finer powers" (*EMF* 126). Sylvain meanwhile presses her to be a socialite and hostess, using her beauty and charm to enhance his own public status. Pulled away from her genuine self, Mariana starts to collapse emotionally and then physically. Finding herself again an outcast, Mariana "relapsed into a fever, and died" (*EMF* 129). In other words, the advancement of women could not be attained unless the husband's role in marriage was reformed.

Fuller thus closes the "Mariana" section of *Summer on the Lakes* with a remarkable meditation on the fate of the American nation, now failing without principled leadership. This is an important signal of her turning her attention toward politics. The nation must have, she writes, a guide who is

> no thin Idealist, no coarse Realist, but a man whose eye reads the heavens while his feet step firmly on the ground, and his hands are strong and dexterous for the use of human implements. A man religious, virtuous, and—sagacious; a man of universal sympathies, but self-possessed; a man who knows the region of emotion, though he is not its slave; a man to whom this world is no mere spectacle, or fleeting shadow, but a great solemn game to be played with good heed, for its stakes are of eternal value, yet who, if his own play be true, heeds not what he loses by the falsehood of others. A man who hives from the past, yet knows that its honey can but moderately avail him; whose comprehensive eye scans the present, neither infatuated with its golden lures, nor chilled with its many ventures; who possesses prescience, as the wise man must, but not so far as to be driven mad to-day by the gift which discerns to-morrow. When there is such a man for America, the thought that urges her on will be expressed. (*EMF* 132)

Fuller's reflection here seems a prophecy of Lincoln, who would guide the nation through the difficult years to come.

"Magnetic influences"

Fuller's second narrative, an essay on *Die Seherin von Prevorst*, differs significantly from the story of Mariana. They share a gendered focus, however, suggesting that "The Great Lawsuit" continued to simmer in her thinking. In Frederica Hausse, the subject of Justinus Kerner's 1829 biography, Fuller again presents a woman destroyed by the extraordinary capacity of her perception. She has been deemed a "Seeress" because of her unusual "susceptibility of magnetic influences" (*EMF* 145), a receptivity with the power to set her in conflict with her family and her society. Like Mariana, she feels too deeply and sees too far.

Fuller explained her discussion of the book as a relief from the fatigue of travel, writing, "The book I had brought with me was in strong contrast with the life around me" (*EMF* 144–55). Her frank confession of being an author longing for relief from the very subject she was describing was an amusing narrative tactic, calling on her readers to recognize the potential shortcomings of traveling. Fuller alerted her readers that she was taking them in an unusual direction but deemed it worth the effort. "Very strange was this vision of an exalted and sensitive existence," she wrote of Kerner's book. It "seemed to invade the next sphere, in contrast with the spontaneous, instinctive life, so healthy and so near the ground I had been surveying" (*EMF* 144–55). Fuller was likely one of the first—and one of the few—Americans to read this as yet untranslated "thick and heavy volume, written with true German patience." She regarded this Seeress, however, as "one of the most remarkable cases of high nervous excitement" in recent years, and Kerner's book an important account from a reliable source of the "phenomena of clairvoyance and susceptibility of magnetic influences" (*EMF* 145).

Frederica Hausse's "high nervous excitement" linked her to Mariana, and the descriptions of her "sensibility to magnetic and ghostly influences" (*EMF* 150) were a resource for one of Fuller's deepest interests, the strongly gendered conception of magnetism.[6] "The electrical, the magnetic element in woman has not been fairly developed at any period," she wrote in "The Great Lawsuit." "Everything might be expected from it; [woman] has far more of it than man," she observed (*GL* 38).

Magnetism, electricity, mesmerism, the séance, ether, the raptures of spiritual ecstasy—these were terms for an energy that brought an individual's physical responsiveness into encounters that appeared to be beyond matter.[7] The Seeress was, as Fuller believed, an embodiment of those with connections to the transcendent. She possessed a power that could be shared in interaction with others as a release from imprisoning materiality. Fuller held that such magnetism had social as well as spiritual effects. Fuller brought the Seeress into *Summer on the Lakes* as an example of feminine strength, bolstering the feminist argument that she developed in "The Great Lawsuit." As Christina Zwarg puts it, "Fuller turned Kerner's narrative into a position paper of social critique" (Zwarg 116). The Seeress's strength was also her weakness. Following Kerner's text, Fuller portrayed the Seeress as a woman whose "life of feeling had been too powerful in her childhood" (*EMF* 151), subjecting her to frequent illness and growing weakness as an adult. When Kerner took her as his patient she was near death, almost completely wasted by poor medical treatment and the increasingly strenuous effects of what Kerner termed "the excessive activity of brain that disordered her whole system." Having been "affected so variously and powerfully by magnetic means in the first years of her illness she had now no life more," and found strength only in "what she borrowed from others." As Fuller summarized her condition, she lived "in a great state of weakness, and more in the magnetic and clairvoyant than in the natural human state" (*EMF* 156).

A victim of severe migraine headaches and pain from a pronounced curvature of the spine, Fuller had sought healing in mesmerism, a theory of the interactions between the mind and body which swept across England and America in the 1830s, making an enormous impact. Alison Winters has described mesmerism's massive following in Victorian Britain, linking it with its scientific contemporaries, electricity and magnetism. Mesmerism was one of the signs of the opening frontiers in the understanding of the interwoven nature of mind and body.[8] During much of the time when Fuller was engaged with her friendship circle, she was dealing with debilitating pain and gradually developing an understanding that pain had both physical and psychic dimensions. Anton Mesmer's theories, popularized as "animal magnetism," emphasized the flow of magnetic energy. His demonstrations of the impact of this energy generated an alteration in physical states and induced hypnotic trances. To Fuller, it was clear that these new explorations of the reception of magnetic forces related to the mystical powers of Novalis's health-bearing carbuncle, an object of both material beauty and unseen spiritual energies.

Fuller saw this conception of the electrically charged natural world as an extension of spirituality, encompassing the body and displacing the deeply entrenched mind-body duality of Christianity. Mesmerism in this sense suggested that the invigorated body was the counterpart of the exhilarated or ecstatic mind. She was not a rabid believer in clairvoyance and other paranormal powers, but she was engaged by the possibility of new discoveries. Her interest in the Seeress indicated her openness, her recognition that all knowledge had not yet been discovered and that all forms of perception were not as yet understood. While she recognized an imbalance in the Seeress, she followed Kerner in regarding her condition as a potential gift, not a burden or disability. Fuller perceived her as a misunderstood and maligned prodigy who offered glimpses beyond the capacity of ordinary men and women. Fuller expressed this view by using evolutionary concepts to frame the Seeress as an example of the higher phases of human consciousness to come. She described the human brain as an "immense galvanic battery" and praised it as an "engine, not only of perception, but of conception and consecutive thought" (*EMF* 165).

"Shall go in December"

After she returned from the West, William Henry Channing welcomed Fuller on her arrival in New York, and she soon visited his Christian Union church. This new congregation was Channing's endeavor to bring socialism and liberal Christian spirituality together in the "fulfillment of man's destiny upon earth" (*CU* 3). Fuller's long correspondence with Channing had been important for both, and his reform work would soon become enormously helpful to Fuller's advocacy for women.

Fuller published *Summer on the Lakes* on June 4, 1844, an accomplishment that opened a new phase for her. She had planned to write a book after she returned from the trip west, and as Megan Marshall writes, she "had talked her way into desk privileges at Harvard's library in palatial Gore Hall," an institution "never before opened to a woman for anything more than an impromptu tour" (Marshall 211). She got further into the project in early April, when Channing invited her to a New York Fourierist convention. She spoke there with Horace Greeley, editor of the *New-York Tribune*, who had been impressed with the "Great Lawsuit" essay. With his encouragement and publication savvy, she was able to make her memorial of the western excursion into her first book. Greeley spoke to Fuller about becoming the *Tribune*'s literary editor during their discussion of *Summer on the Lakes* (Capper 2:165). His willingness to advise her and promote her work was a huge boost for Fuller, who was struggling to find a secure direction.

An entry in Fuller's 1844 journal leaps off the page to suggest her anguish and sense of desolation only a few weeks after the successful publication of her book. "O I need some help," she wrote, and then quickly corrected herself. "No I need a full a godlike embrace from some sufficient love. I know not why, but the wound of my heart has reopened yesterday & today. My head aches."[9] She had thought that her wounds from the friendship circle might be cured in the West, and as her journal convincingly shows, a new friend had appeared during the trip. He was James Freeman Clarke's younger brother from Chicago, William. He and Fuller seem to have made strong impressions on each other and had exchanged letters after the trip. Clarke visited Boston in the early spring of 1844, and as Martha Berg and Alice Perry note, "their relationship intensified" (J 1844 44). This reunion did not flourish as Fuller had hoped, it appears, because "Clarke may also have developed some kind of relationship" with Caroline Sturgis (J 1844 48). Before he prepared to leave Boston in June, he sent Fuller a gentle poem that was clearly a good-bye (Capper 2:137).

While William Clarke may well have been the figure behind Fuller's desire for "a full a godlike embrace," her suffering reveals the burden of loneliness that she had carried for several years. Powerful though she was intellectually, she yearned for deep spiritual unions in her friendships, male and female. "I cannot write well now," she lamented. "Yet feel the need of writing." Sturgis had been a crucial support for her after the blow of the Ward-Barker marriage, and in another journal entry, Fuller wrote of a visit in which, sharing a bed, "we both went to sleep & kept waking now and then." Fuller remembered this as "a time of deep life" that "had permanent effect on my life," a closeness that "could not be spoken of unless in verse" (J 1844 56).[10] These drives were in part physical, but they also pushed Fuller into deeper analysis of the nature of sexuality and of gender. As Marshall expresses it, Fuller struggled with the sense "that male and female were united in her," and while starved for a close bond, she feared that "carnal love of either man or woman" would "lead to personal disunion, dis-integration" (Marshall 258). These inner struggles, however, strengthened her intellectual growth, and she began to develop a deeper sense of the meaning of a new definition of the human. Her emotional anxieties had made Fuller resist Greeley's job offer in April, but her hesitation to move to New York also reflected her sense that to work at the *Tribune* would entail a change of identities for her—from author, expert on Goethe, and rising literary figure to newspaper journalist. The job that Greeley proposed, as Larry Reynolds has pointed out, "represented a lowering that both she and her Concord friends had difficulty adjusting to."[11] Moving from Boston to New York to work for a newspaper was in this sense a challenging proposition for her. But when Greeley came unexpectedly to see her in Cambridge in mid-September, Fuller decided, cautiously, to take the chance. Recording the moment in her journal, she wrote: "I engaged to go to N. Y. & at least try it. Shall go in December. I now feel quite easy in doing it" (J 1844 118).[12] Part of Fuller's satisfaction with her decision came from her planning a new book. She made the next two months her own.

Few sabbaticals have been as productive as the seven weeks in the fall of 1844 that Fuller spent completing *Woman in the Nineteenth Century*. Fuller left Boston and settled in Fishkill Landing, a resort north of New York on the Hudson.[13] It was a beautiful writing retreat, but not a total seclusion. Caroline Sturgis, who herself was now living principally in New

York, traveled with her, and she had several other visitors during the stay, but she found her best voice there.

The sadness and injustice of women's subjugation, and the wasted potential of their capability and creativity, bristled in Fuller during those weeks. Her social and political outlook had developed extensively in the fifteen months between completing "The Great Lawsuit" and beginning *Woman in the Nineteenth Century*. Traveling into the American frontier had opened her eyes to the hideous mistreatment of the Native Americans and shown her the ruthless greed and chauvinism of the westward annexation. Her suspicion that the frontier offered little hope for progressive reform had been fully confirmed. While she had seen no easy pathway to justice for the people there, she returned east to find an energetic experiment in Channing's efforts to formulate a religious and socially active Associationism. Channing represented for her a transcendentalist alternative to Emerson and his doctrine of the intellectual responsibility of the scholar. But by August of 1844, even Emerson had taken a major progressive step. With the antislavery atmosphere in Boston, and especially Concord, heating steadily, he had closely read Thomas Clarkson's account of the British abolition of the slave trade and James A. Thome and J. Horace Kimball's book on the British emancipation of slaves in the West Indies. Sobered by what he found, he wrote one of his most moving and profound addresses, "Emancipation in the British West Indies." He delivered it in Concord on August first. Fuller was there to hear it. A week before the event Fuller had commented on a somewhat troubling conversation she had had with him. "Waldo came in & talked his transcendental fatalism a little. Then went away, declaring he should not come again till he was less stupid. I had as lief he would sit here and not say a word, but it would be impossible to make him understand that" (J 1844 93). What she heard a week later was far different. "But Waldo's oration, O that was great heroic, calm, sweet, fair," she wrote. "I felt excited to new life and a nobler emulation by Waldo this day. Yes: it is deeply tragic on one side, my relation to him, but on the other, how noble how dear! If not an immortal relation, it makes me more immortal." Her only hope was to "keep both sides duly balanced in my mind" (J 1844 107–8). This "heroic, calm, sweet, fair" Emerson remained a support for Fuller's continuing advocacy for social change.

The deepest impact on Fuller's expansion of *Woman in the Nineteenth Century*, however, was made by the imprisoned women she encountered in New York, with the help of Georgiana Bruce and Channing. Fuller met Bruce on an October 1843 visit to Brook Farm and quickly became a friend and adviser to her. When Bruce moved from Brook Farm to work with the reformer Eliza Farnham at Sing Sing prison, she stayed in touch with Fuller and sent her journals written by some of the female inmates. These were intended for Fuller's projected novel, a Goethean "Lehrjahre for women" (*FL* 3:221) that would depict the nature of female experience and growth.[14] Arriving just as Fuller was beginning her reworking of "The Great Lawsuit," the journals of the imprisoned women made a deep impression on her. "These women in their degradation express most powerfully the present wants of the sex at large," she told Bruce. "What blasphemes in them must fret and murmur in the perfumed boudoir, for society beats with one great heart" (*FL* 3:223). By late October she and Channing had arranged a trip to Sing Sing, where she was able to speak to the women directly. As she wrote afterwards: "They were among the so called worst but nothing could be more decorous than their conduct, and frank too. All passed much as in one of my Boston Classes" (*FL* 3:237). What Fuller found in these women was hope. Whatever their circumstance, they had the capability of learning and the self-possession to change and grow. They would respond to the message she was preparing.

"Self-reliance and self-impulse"

Returning to her essay, Fuller wrote that there now was a "THRONG of symptoms which denote the present tendency to a crisis in the life of woman" (*EMF* 313). Her earlier essay had presented a compelling case for women from the deepest historical roots of civilization. She now addressed her own day and moment and did so with urgency. She had closed "The Great Lawsuit" with a discussion of her beloved Goethe, "the great mind which gave itself absolutely to the leadings of truth," and a thinker who had provided "his wonderful sight as to the prospect and wants of women" (GL 47). As she took up the "crisis" that she now felt, she returned to Goethe, adding Swedenborg and Fourier as "prophets of the coming age" (*EMF* 313) of justice for women. Her comparison of Goethe and Fourier, presented as a nimble debate, signified her growing regard for Fourier, but also revealed her skepticism toward a plan "to change mankind" through an "arrangement of groups and series" (*EMF* 315). Fourier had argued that no social progress could be made until the oppression of women was ended. For Fuller, however, his mechanistic realignment of human relations carried less promise than Goethe's ability to recognize and creatively represent women with strength and self-possession. "He aims at a pure self-subsistence, and free development of any powers with which [women] may be gifted by nature as much for them as for men. They are units, addressed as souls" (*EMF* 317). To say that his female literary characters reflect "pure self-subsistence," and were to be addressed as souls, meant that Goethe glimpsed through these characters a new world of equality in which every woman could claim her full potential, without the resistance or unwanted direction of men.

Speaking of "self-subsistence," and later of "self-impulse," terms that have been little noted in the commentary on transcendentalism, Fuller was able to focus on the particularly complex impediments that women faced in their path to self-development. "Now there is no woman," she declared, "only an overgrown child" (*EMF* 347), a charge that echoed her own earlier experience of self-recognition. This cutting appraisal of her own sex may seem harsh, but it pointedly illustrated the atmosphere of crisis that centered on the difficult "change from girlhood" and development "to self-possessed, wise, and graceful womanhood" (*EMF* 313). She did not find in the women of her own day the self-subsistence or independent wholeness that she found in the women of Goethe's writings. "I have urged upon the sex self-subsistence in its two forms of self-reliance and self-impulse, because I believe them to be the needed means of the present juncture" (*EMF* 346).

Self-reliance, the title Emerson chose for his best-known literary work, was not a coincidental word choice on Fuller's part. She felt that self-reliance as Emerson had presented it did not adequately account for the nineteenth-century woman's effort to realize her potential. At first reading, it is unclear what Fuller meant by contrasting self-reliance with "self-impulse," a term that I have found in none of her other works nor elsewhere. Self-impulse was one form of self-subsistence, Fuller wrote, a characteristic that either supplemented self-reliance in the Emersonian sense or fulfilled the aims of Goethean self-subsistence in a new way. Fuller coined the term "self-impulse" to resist the suppression of female creativity and decision-making. In several passages of *Woman in the Nineteenth Century*, she condemned the obstacles that women faced and insisted that "we only ask of men to remove arbitrary barriers" (*EMF* 345). In a demand that has been somewhat less noted, she also urged that the steps toward women's advance should be determined by women. Self-impulse, as Fuller used it, meant the welling up of purpose from within. It meant not just the right to choose but the will to exercise choice. What gave *Woman in the Nineteenth Century* its burn, we might say, was Fuller's clear insistence that women were calling not only for the right of equality but also for the right to decide what equality actually was. "I believe that, at the present, women are the best helpers of one another," she wrote. "Let them think; let them act; till they know what they need" (*EMF* 344–45). It was not that women now knew what steps they must take, but rather that they were the ones who must learn for themselves what those steps must be. Some men, she recognized, "would like to do more." She felt, however, that "it needs for woman to show herself in her native dignity, to teach them how to help her." The advice of men was unreliable since "their minds are so encumbered by tradition" (*EMF* 345).

Because Emerson was not thinking in terms of gender, there is nothing like Fuller's term "self-impulse" in his "Self-Reliance." He did, however, come somewhat closer to Fuller's mode of thinking in "Circles," in which he described his concept of the soul's unceasing impulse for growth. Fuller shared Emerson's belief in the continually developing soul. Goethe's self-subsistent women were presented as "souls," she had written. She emphasized the importance of the developing soul throughout *Woman in the Nineteenth Century*, fervently arguing that women had been arrested in their ability to recognize and pursue their own goals and capabilities. "It is for that which is the birthright of every capable being to receive it,—the freedom, the religious, the intelligent freedom of the universe, to use its means; to learn its secret as far as nature enabled them, with God alone for their guide and their judge" (*EMF* 276). Invoking both the laws of nature and the authority of God, she asserted that the hindrance of female development was inexcusable. Her argument was a clear directive for both individuals and institutions to respond to the needs of women's education, and further instruction to women to accept the responsibility of teaching women to seek their fullest selves. "Give the soul free course, let the organization, both of body and mind, be freely developed, and the being will be fit for any and every relation to which it may be called" (*EMF* 298). Fuller's passion and her eloquence are ringing in this call to the furthering of women.

For Fuller, the soul signified the spiritually grounded nature of the deep self, the core of that which signaled both the divine and the fully engaged human. "Let us be wise and not impede the soul," she wrote, fighting entrenched resistance to widening possibilities for women's vocations and social roles. "Let her work as she will," she argued, referring to both the soul's power to bring women forward and to the women who ached for new work. Resisting the assumption that some tasks, responsibilities, or creative opportunities are masculine and others feminine, she declared: "Let us have one creative energy, one incessant revelation. Let it take what form it will, and let us not bind it by the past to man or woman, black or white" (*EMF* 311).

Fuller's inclusion of the racial implications of her theory of women's equality is clear in this call for a fully egalitarian society. Her sense of the free soul, unfettered by the past, moving with "creative energy" and "incessant revelation," captured the simultaneous energies that she felt in late 1844. Working with Channing and Bruce, Fuller had met imprisoned women in New York and conversed with them, recognizing them as victims of a social order that was corrupt.[15] These women, she realized, were the "sold and polluted slaves of men," who had experienced an oppression that mirrored the repugnant legal slavery of the American South. Protecting the victimizers, Fuller contemptuously wrote, were "the legislator and the man of the world," who said, "This must be; it cannot be helped; it is a necessary accompaniment of civilization" (*EMF* 319–20). Such easy tolerance of the damage to and destruction of these women and men, Fuller argued, could not be allowed in a society that was truly civil. "The soul is ever young, ever virgin," she wrote in the closing pages of the book. The strength of the soul was finally indestructible. "It is not woman, but the law of right, the law of growth, that speaks in us, and demands the perfection of each being in its kind, apple as apple, woman as woman" (*EMF* 347).

"The great work of popular education"

By the time *Woman in the Nineteenth Century* was published on February 16, 1845, Fuller had begun to establish herself as one of the *New-York Tribune*'s key writers. In the same way that her work for *The Dial* unleashed an outpouring of creative expression, the *Tribune*, with its demand for constant and varied writing, brought out Fuller's extraordinary apprehension of human experience. It took several weeks before Fuller began to attune herself fully to the punishing routines of the newspaper, but with Greeley's patience and support she gradually took her place.[16] She got along famously with Greeley. "Mr. Greeley is in many ways very interesting for me to know," she wrote. "He teaches me things, which my own influence on those, who have hitherto approached me, has prevented me from learning. In our business and friendly relations, we are on terms of solid good-will and mutual respect. With the exception of my own mother, I think him the most disinterestedly generous person I have ever known" (*FL* 4:40). As she developed the daily front-page column that Greeley had confidently given her, it seemed as if she had found the medium through which she could express both her aesthetic discernment and her political awareness.

Through her own reading, and the intense supplications of Channing, Fuller was already cautiously moving toward Fourierism when she decided to move to New York. In Greeley, however, she found an active figure in national electoral politics, who was both prominent in the Whig Party and a dedicated Fourierist. Philip Gura's reassessment of Greeley among the American romantic reformers emphasized the unusual blending of Whig principles of family values, conscientious work, and orderly social procedures with the Fourierist concern for suitable labor for all. The concern for the plight of workers, which grew out of Greeley's penurious childhood, had been sharpened by the ravaging of employment in the Panic of 1837. Greeley used Fourier to critique "man's flawed economic arrangements" and "centered on Fourier's signal concept, the doctrine of Association" as the path to cooperative economic relations among communities.[17]

Fuller was the *Tribune*'s literary editor, but she quickly transformed the role into that of an all-encompassing cultural critic, inspired by New York's vast promise and its grim decadence. Her earlier worries about lowering herself by moving into journalism never surfaced. She wrote 250 articles in twenty months before leaving for Europe in August 1846.[18] This is impressive numerically, but the real impact of Fuller's journalistic work was in its variety and intellectual range. Judith Mattson Bean and Joel Myerson have provided a "Topical Table of Contents" of the eighty-eight published articles, which included "American Literature," "British Literature," "Cultural and Social Criticism," "European Languages and Literature," "Literary Criticism and Genres of Literature," and "Music and Art" (*MFC* ix–xxi). Within these broad categories, Fuller commented on "belles lettres, popular literature, gift books, history, biography, travel writing, textbooks, pamphlets, public reports, and periodicals" (*MFC* xxxvi). This variety, during a period in which women were writing and publishing widely on many subjects and in many genres, allowed her to continue her support for the cause of women in a prominent and authoritative way. Her writings were, for the most part, far from politically partisan, but she brought front-page attention to the writings or activities of reformists such as Lydia Maria Child, Eliza Farnham, and Catharine Sedgwick. Greeley, who was a stronger socialist than Fuller, allowed her complete independence in her work.

Perhaps the best indication of Fuller's critical intellect early in her Tribune work was her assessment of Emerson's *Essays: Second Series*, a fascinating performance in which she seeks to augment Emerson's national stature while more subtly indicating the limitations of his leadership, and of her discipleship. Barbara Packer terms it "a gesture of filial piety toward and a declaration of independence from Emerson."[19] Emerson's book was published at precisely the moment when Fuller had begun revising "The Great Lawsuit" into Woman in the Nineteenth Century. The delicacy of Fuller's task should be noted. This volume included Emerson's greatest and most personal essay, "Experience," in which he made public reference to the loss of his son Waldo, a child whom Fuller knew and loved. It also included "The Poet," an important essay that would become central in the American canon.

Despite her troubled relationship with Emerson, Fuller knew him as a force for good and an ally in the causes of public enlightenment and progressive social reform. Yet Emerson himself had always preached that a perfect frankness, even "the rude truth," was the tribute one friend owed another.[20] The arrival of his new book thus became both an opportunity and a burden for Fuller. She knew that she could give his book the wide exposure of a *Tribune* review, but she also understood a further responsibility: to show both to him and to his growing readership the new and more politically engaged direction his movement should now take. Fuller did not write to Emerson in detail about his book until after she had drafted her revised version of *Woman in the Nineteenth Century*. Her praise was direct: "It will be a companion through my life" (*FL* 3:243).

Fuller begins her review essay by addressing what has become an enduring and complex issue of Emerson criticism, his relationship to his American readership and lecture audience. Emerson, in Fuller's view, has not compromised in either the subject matter or the style of his work and has thus set an example of intellectual integrity in establishing his public reputation. The typical American reader, she observes, has been injured not only by the frontier conditions of American life but also "by a large majority of writers and speakers, who lend all their efforts to flatter corrupt tastes and mental indolence, instead of feeling it their prerogative and their duty to admonish the community of the danger and arouse it to nobler energy" (*MFC* 1–2). Emerson has succeeded by standing against the caustic energies of vulgarized popular discourse, which, if succumbed to, make it "inevitable" that "Literature and Art must become daily more degraded" (*MFC* 2). Fuller's praise of Emerson, however, is the prelude to a perceptive critique that signals the ascendancy of the reformist emphasis of transcendentalism. She finds a fundamental inadequacy in what we might call Emerson's range of concern. "The human heart complains of inadequacy, either in the nature or experience of the writer, to represent its full vocation and its deeper needs" (*MFC* 5). This universalized "human heart" is very close, of course, to Fuller's own, and her references to "experience," "vocation," and "deeper needs" originate in her transforming but nevertheless incomplete relationship with Emerson.

This "inadequacy" or "under-development" is suggested by a problem that is stylistic, in the first instance, but symptomatic of something larger. "This writer," she asserts, "has never written one good work, if such a work be one where the whole commands more attention than the parts" (*MFC* 5). Fuller makes Emerson's facility with the aphorism or brief passage a symptom of his inability to master the whole. The result is that one reads Emerson with a sense of restriction or confinement. He takes his reader to great heights of thought only to awaken recognition of the possibility of an even more comprehensive view of reality. "We miss what we expect in the work of the great poet, or the great philosopher," Fuller declares, "the liberal air of all the zones: the glow, uniform yet various in tint, which is given to a body by free circulation of the heart's blood from the hour of birth" (*MFC* 5). Fuller, no doubt, has Goethe in mind as an example of the "great" poets or philosophers who have achieved something more akin to this comprehensive and "liberal" air. Goethe's cosmopolitanism, and his remarkably wide range of interests and endowments, traits that in some respects made him problematic to many nineteenth-century Americans, signified his commitment to lived experience, the embodiment of philosophy in life. Listen to Fuller's description of Emerson carefully, noting her sense that he lacks "the glow, uniform yet various in tint, which is given to a body by free circulation of the heart's blood from the hour of birth." She is calling Emerson bloodless, a spectral thinker whose philosophy is too far detached from life. Fuller has found in Emerson's cool, in his highmindedness, the central problem of both his philosophy and his life. Her wish for him, part spiteful but mostly compassionate, is that he might somehow be ruffled, perhaps profoundly so. If Emerson's philosophy, she reasons, has partaken too much of the heavens, making his thinking seem thin and unsubstantial, perhaps it should be brought back to earth and made strong again.

Fuller's *Tribune* work in the following months intensified her awareness of the troubling social realities in the bustling city. She became much more disquieted by the social injustices arising from class divisions, and she looked for practical ways to redress them. She began to bring moral authority and intellectual clarity to bear on the brutal social world that she found. She became, through her practice of a rudimentary form of investigative reporting and public advocacy, "New York's public conscience," in Jeffrey Steele's apt phrase (Steele 259). And while offering her readers reviews of Emerson, Hawthorne, Longfellow, and Poe, she also reviewed the annual reports of prisons, asylums, and schools for the deaf, using her front-page *Tribune* slot to keep such institutions, and the problems with which they were wrestling, before the public eye.

Fuller thus came to see more clearly the ethical imperative behind the building of secure institutions that could advance social justice. Her discussion of progressive reform returned repeatedly to the fundamental principle of the integrity and worth of every human life. The treatment and institutional care of the mentally ill is an act of both moral principle and social justice. She found much to weep for, however. Her article "Our City Charities" reported on her visit to the public institutions in New York, including the Bellevue Alms House, the Farm School, and the Asylum for the Insane, where she encountered disturbing evidence of neglect and abuse and confronted the callous social irresponsibility these conditions revealed (*MFC* 98–104). "The aspect of Nature was sad" with a "leaden and lowering" sky when she set out on the visit, Fuller recalled, a darkness that set the mood for a mission to the discarded and forgotten. Such a visit, she explained, was a necessary reminder of the tenuous security of every man and woman. The penitentiary at Blackwell's Island was even more disturbing, "one of the gloomiest scenes that deforms this great metropolis," Fuller wrote. "Never was punishment treated more simply as a social convenience, without regard to pure right, or a hope of reformation" (*MFC* 102). New York had thus constructed, through callous social indifference, a set of conditions whose effect was to destroy the hope of human development.

These desperate conditions did not defeat her underlying hope for reform, but they made her cognizant of the stubborn persistence of certain forms of social injustice, and of the apathy and lack of information that helped to sustain them. "There is no reason why New-York should not become a model for other States in these things," she argued in advocating reformation of the Blackwell's Island Penitentiary. "There is wealth enough, intelligence, and good desire enough, and *surely, need enough*" (MFC 103).[21]

The Margaret Fuller who sailed for Europe in August 1846 could still be considered a transcendentalist. But she was not the same woman who had arrived in New York to write for the *Tribune*. As she began to meet radical intellectuals like Giuseppe Mazzini and Adam Mickiewicz, involved in revolutionary activities, Fuller was confirmed in her understanding that self-development and self-expression necessarily had a political dimension. Her life had indeed changed. The decision to go to New York had opened the world for her.

CHAPTER 5

Young Europe and Its Democracy

"My Genius Wings"

Fuller's move to New York was more than successful; it was a decision that unleashed a stream of thought, writing, and action that she might not otherwise have achieved. Horace Greeley provided her with a new level of self-assurance as a pleased mentor and friend. Of great importance was Greeley's provision of material support—salary, free rent, introduction, and opportunities that opened a new world for her. William Channing's ministry, and the range of open-minded acquaintances it brought, added to Fuller's ability to quickly build a sense of community and shared focus among progressive associates.

Greeley developed the *Tribune* as an international publication and was eager to bring both European politics and European literature to New York. Fuller followed Albert Brisbane at the *Tribune*, an ardent Fourierist who had provided the paper with a steady stream of highly systematized Associationism. While Fuller remained a somewhat cautious advocate of Fourier, she was not taken by Brisbane's dogma. She developed a remarkably varied column that mixed reviews and cultural commentary with politics and social questions, drawing from European news and publications, often in her own translation. She kept the *Tribune* as close to Europe as she could.

At the Fourierist convention in New York of April 1844 where she met Greeley, Fuller also met Rebecca Buffum Spring and her husband, Marcus. Rebecca was a Quaker whose father, Arthur Buffum, was one of the founders and the first president of the New England Anti-Slavery Society. Rebecca too was "an ardent abolitionist, who visited the insurrectionist John Brown in prison" and "petitioned for his release."[1] Close friends of both Greeley and Channing, they shared Fuller's interests in prison reform and Associationism.[2] They would become crucial friends and supporters, soon asking her to accompany them and their nine-year-old son Eddie on a trip to Europe. In exchange for tutoring Eddie, they also proposed to pay some of her expenses, an important offer for Fuller. It was, as Rebecca later wrote, an invitation at which Fuller "cried for joy" (Capper 2:271).

Fuller's "joy," however, does not disclose the storm that was beginning to build as she considered the European trip. "It is now ten years since I was forced to abandon the hope of going at the time when I held my health and mind required it as they never could again," she wrote Samuel Ward. This was the journey on which he met Anna Barker in Switzerland. "Still more I felt that in not going with you at the time when our minds were so in unison, and when I was drawn so strongly towards your peculiar province, I lost what life could never replace. I feel so still" (FL 4:192). The prospect of the coming voyage had awakened in her the anguish of the voyage lost, and with it the romantic wreckage of what Fuller had hoped would be marriage with Ward. She clearly believed she had lost indelible impressions, unique insights, and unattainable wisdom in the now forgone 1836 voyage. She told Ward that she had been deprived of an essential moment of her education, and with it her capacity to fully grasp the world. "At every step I have missed the culture I sought in going, for with me it [was] no scheme of pleasure but the means of needed development. It was what I wanted after my painful youth, and what I was ready to use and be nourished by." This forsaken chance to see Europe, she believed, had crippled her spirit's capacity to fully express itself. The journey "would have given my genius wings and I should have been, not in idea indeed, but in achievement far superior to what I can be now" (FL 4:192).

One further source of distress also weighed on her as she began to prepare for the trip she had so badly wanted—a man named James Nathan.

The fourth volume of Robert N. Hudspeth's edition of Fuller's letters includes some three dozen letters to Nathan, which, as Elizabeth Hardwick described them, "become quite frenzied with that pitiful wonder of the injured person of what she, in this case, might have done wrong."[3] Nathan was an emigrated German who was a successful businessman and banker. Fuller met him soon after settling in New York at a New Year's Eve party and began a correspondence with him—most of the letters were Fuller's—that soon became a closer series of walks, meetings, and long conversations. What she did not know, at least at first, was that Nathan "had a young woman living with him in his apartments" (Marshall 252). When Fuller eventually discovered this, Nathan explained that he had offered help to a poor and incapacitated woman. The dismayed Fuller took him at his word, hoping that their courtship could continue. This remarkable incident stayed unknown for some fifty years, until Fuller's love letters were put up for sale. Although she had demanded them back from Nathan, he had kept the letters instead, leaving them to his son, who then sold them.

It is clear, whatever Fuller saw in him, that she loved him. After losing contact with him for several weeks during their romance, she sent him a lengthy, questioning, somewhat fearful letter on the last day of 1845. "I do not, indeed, feel separated from you," she assured him; "your silences, or the want of personal intercourse does not seem to have that effect at all. When I am alone, your image rises before me, or indeed in the presence of others I sometimes am suddenly lost to them and seem absorbed by this communion" (*FL* 4:179). She would carry this haunted passion with her as she crossed the Atlantic in August 1846. A long-awaited letter from Nathan had given Fuller hope of seeing him in Europe, but what awaited her on her arrival was another letter, announcing his plan to marry a German woman. In what Hudspeth terms "at first fury and then depression" (*FL* 4:10), Fuller began her European trip.[4]

Almost immediately after receiving the letter from Nathan, Fuller traveled with the Springs to Edinburgh and then the Scottish Highlands. She left Edinburgh in a nearly traumatic state. As Hudspeth relates, "Rebecca Spring, who knew of Fuller's love for Nathan and of his rejection of her, later remembered that, to their surprise, the deeply despondent Fuller stayed outside on the top of the coach in a driving rain as they headed for Loch Katrine and Ben Lomond" (FL 4:10). Fuller was carrying a burden of piercing misery as they rode to the area below the mountain. In the opening of her dispatch to the *Tribune* about the journey from Edinburgh, Fuller made one comment that requires some consideration. Explaining her preference for traveling by coach rather than train, she noted, "I have been everywhere on the top of the coach, even one day of drenching rain, and enjoy it highly."[5] Written a week after the tearful departure from Edinburgh, Fuller's comment was likely aimed at the Springs.

They stayed at Loch Katrine, near the summit of Ben Lomond. On "a day of ten thousand" (SG 74), as Fuller praised it, she set out with Marcus Spring to make the rather demanding four-hour hike to the summit. Reaching the peak at dusky nightfall, she encountered "beauty and grandeur such as imagination never painted" (SG 74). The view from Ben Lomond's peak was *transcendental*. "You see around you no plain ground, but on every side constellations or groups of hills exquisitely dressed in the soft purple of the heather, amid which gleam the lakes like eyes that tell the secrets of the earth and drink in those of the heavens" (SG 74). "Peak beyond peak," she wrote, as if gasping in prolonged awe, "caught from the shifting light all the colors of the prism, and on the farthest angel companies seemed hovering in their glorious white robes" (SG 74). Presenting the view from the peak as heavenly, Fuller dramatized the entire walk as a pilgrimage, a journey toward spiritual awakening and self-understanding. That journey took a turn, however, when she called out to Marcus and discovered that she had lost her way on the descent and had become separated from him.

This was the moment when the pilgrimage became a struggle for survival. She attempted to walk directly down toward the hotel but found "I would sink up to my knees in bog," exhausting herself as she scuffled back up the hill (SG 75). After much effort she glimpsed the distant hotel and the lake beside it in the dim light. What follows this discovery is a gripping description of her entrapment on the hillside near a roaring waterfall, as the night chilled and darkened, and she pondered her fate. In moving toward the hotel, she had encountered "a high heathery hill" called "The Tongue," surrounded on three sides by rapidly flowing streams. She could not reach the hotel without fording one of the steams. "It looked very deep, and I felt afraid; it looked so deep in the dim twilight." She tested the stream by throwing in a stone, but "it sounded very hollow, and I was afraid to jump." That test saved her. As she learned afterwards, the stream was indeed deep and "the bed of the torrent full of sharp stones." She settled on the hill in a state of exhaustion, seeing distantly below her the inn, "a light that looked about as big as a pin's head" (SG 75).

Though she had avoided the treacherous stream, she believed that she "should not live through the night, or if I did, live always a miserable invalid." Fuller's fear that she had saved herself at the riverside only to die on the mountain slope was understandable, and it spurred her again to take positive control of her situation. Realizing that there was "no chance to keep myself warm by walking," she instead pushed herself "to keep in motion the whole of that long night." Battling for alertness, she transformed her fear into a reflective, sustaining meditation. "The mental experience of the time," which she remembered as "most precious and profound," engendered "the birth of thoughts beyond what the common sunlight will ever call to being" (SG 76). Brought to the edge of life, Fuller embraced it.

As the night wore on, Fuller observed the ghostlike fog "floating slowly and gracefully" with the "great body of mists," bearing "a kiss pervasively cold as that of Death." Even so, she refused to resign herself passively to the dark's "cold, spirit-like breathing." She was able to persist in her wakeful resistance against the cold until "at last the moon rose," and she knew that she would survive. While she took the moonrise as an assurance that she could now rest, having "weathered out so much of the night," its appearance also carried significant symbolic importance (SG 76). As Jeffrey Steele points out, Fuller, in other stories, had employed the moon and its light as emblems of female creativity, power, and independence. These works "constructed models of independent womanhood challenging the period's platitudes about proper female thought and behavior" (Steele 72).[6] Fuller's recognition of the moon's appearance in "Lost on Ben Lomond" can also be seen as an episode of female perception, determination, judgment, and self-reliance.

Despite a thick mist, dawn finally arrived, and Fuller continued her search for a crossing point on the river, then kept walking toward the inn until at last she was found and taken home. The account that she sent to the *Tribune* was no doubt an unexpected and captivating work of journalism. It was also an implicit declaration of self-renewal that transformed her European travels into a genuinely open quest for accord and purpose. It would be a stronger, more self-possessed woman who arrived in London in October.[7] She had decided to end her connection with Nathan and asked him to return her letters. Though he refused, she continued in London with a refreshed feeling of resolve. She had gained lunar energy from Ben Lomond's moonlight, and within a month would find in the Italian freedom fighter Giuseppe Mazzini a person with the intellect, principles, purpose, and connections to open Europe to her.

"She has suffered—she has revolted"

Before leaving for Europe, Fuller had assisted the Danish writer Harro Harring in his publication of *Dolores: A Novel of South America*. The novel portrayed Giuseppe Mazzini as an international revolutionary hero. Harring, who had moved to London before Fuller arrived, arranged for her to meet with Mazzini on October 24. She was able to see Mazzini again two weeks later at a gathering that would firmly bond her to Mazzini and his cause.[8] Mazzini was conducting a celebration for one of his most successful programs, the Italian Gratuitous School, through which he had undertaken to educate the many orphaned and abandoned Italian children who were living in exile in London. This school had made an enormously positive impact on British support of Italian freedom.[9] Mazzini, who quickly befriended Fuller, asked her to speak to an audience of Italian school children and many of the liberal-minded Londoners who supported the school. Italy, Fuller reminded her audience, "has bestowed on the rest of the world" the artistic works that "awaken the love of the beautiful and the good, and thus refine the human soul." Once recognizing its importance, "can anyone, capable of thought on the subject, be indifferent to the emancipation of this fair land from [its] present degradation?"[10] How prophetic these words would soon prove to be. Fuller's early connection in London with Mazzini gave her a sense of the burning desire for emancipation in Italy and elsewhere in Europe.

Fuller soon praised Mazzini in a *Tribune* article that revealed the deepening of a democratic globalism that was shaping her political attitude. Mazzini embodied a transnational posture, even though he was thoroughly nationalistic. Addressing her *Tribune* readers, Fuller declared, "One of the most interesting things I have seen here or elsewhere" was "the school for poor Italian boys, sustained and taught by a few of their exiled compatriots, and especially by the mind and efforts of Mazzini" (SG 98). This was a gesture of community needed worldwide, and Mazzini's name was "well known" among supporters of "the cause of human freedom" (SG 98). She looked to Mazzini's cause and his methods as a worldwide endeavor that must become American as well. Mazzini's work was of "universal interest in all nations and places where Man, understanding his inheritance, strives to throw off an arbitrary rule and establish a state of things where he shall be governed as becomes a man by his own conscience and intelligence," and "where he may speak the truth as it rises in his mind" (SG 98).

Mazzini, as she described him here, appeared to be working from the same principles that she herself had advocated in her argument for the liberation of women. Fuller had in fact encountered Mazzini at the peak of his articulation of a democratic theory that was rooted in resistance to the Austrian oppression of Italy. He had been exiled in Britain since 1837, and it might be said that he had actually been exiled to the Reading Room of the British Museum. His linguistic abilities and his voluminous reading matched those of Fuller, and he used the name Joseph as a sign of his fluent English. He had, during his long exile, found friendship and support from several prominent Londoners, including Thomas Carlyle and his wife, Jane Welsh Carlyle, who became, as he wrote, "the woman I value most in England."[11]

Fuller's arrival in London occurred near the end of the so-called Post Office Scandal, a prolonged political squabble that had enlarged Mazzini's public recognition and his popularity. He had discovered that the British home secretary, Sir James Graham, had secretly opened his correspondence after a request from authorities in Austria, who regarded Mazzini, accurately, as a dangerous threat to their hold on Italy. Mazzini, outraged, petitioned the British Parliament over the meddling with his mail, igniting several months of heated argument in the London press and gaining him favor from a British public who held the privacy of their letters sacred. During this scandal, Carlyle provided a ringing testament to *The Times*, calling Mazzini "a man of genius and virtue, a man of sterling veracity, humanity, and nobleness of mind," among the rare individuals "worthy to be called martyr souls."[12] Carlyle and Mazzini were far from agreement on politics, but they had a strong mutual respect.

Despite his disagreements with Mazzini, Carlyle recognized that he was much more a theorist than a soldier. "Great revolutions are the work of principles rather than of bayonets," Mazzini wrote in his "Manifesto to Young Italy," a call to action that was also a philosophical credo. Great revolutions, he continued, "are first achieved in the moral, then in the material sphere. Bayonets are truly powerful when they assert or maintain a right. Now, the rights and duties of society spring from a profound moral sense that has taken root in the majority."[13]

Mazzini believed that such revolutions could achieve their aims only if they had the support of a significant majority of a population who understood the rights that had been denied them and were willing to use force if necessary to claim them. Italy, a divided country ruled by a foreign power, faced a particularly difficult course in its efforts for self-rule, and in his manifesto, he laid out the necessities for its victory. "Any true progress will be fatally impossible in Italy, until every effort at emancipation shall proceed along the three inseparable bases of unity, liberty, and independence" (Recchia and Urbinati 34). The Italians, in other words, must first come together as a unified nation, then defeat Austrian rule and learn how to govern themselves as independent citizens. This final step of education was crucial, he felt, and his advocacy for democratic principles became a key focus of his numerous writings.

Mazzini's political vision was not limited to Italy. He saw democracy as a force that would thrive throughout Europe, generating a populace who would guarantee the rule of egalitarian principles on the continent.[14] He was in this sense both a fierce patriot and a cosmopolitan thinker. In an 1847 essay, "Nationalism and Cosmopolitanism," he critiqued both the "absolute kings" who defined a nation as their own, and also the socialist advocates of "Saint-Simonianism and communism" who wholly neglected the idea of a nation in their thinking. "When we speak of Nationality," he explained, "it is of Nationality such as the *Peoples*, free and brotherly associated, will conceive it" (Recchia and Urbinati 59). He believed that the emancipation of an oppressed people was impossible without "making them fully aware of their existence and their Nationality." Nationhood was, in a crucial way, a form of self-knowledge and self-respect. For a potential leader to see or treat the citizens otherwise was futile. "It is to ask the Peoples to work without assigning a part to them; it is to demand that the work be done while actually *breaking the instrument* for its fulfillment" (Recchia and Urbinati 62). Liberating change, he argued, is dependent on the cultivation of self-awareness and social awakening that accorded closely with Fuller's feminist efforts in her Conversations and her work with imprisoned women.[15]

In the short time she had in London, Fuller befriended Mazzini and left for Paris assured that their bond was lasting. She and the courageous Springs even agreed to smuggle Mazzini into Italy with them, a plan that was eventually abandoned when Mazzini himself recognized the danger. He had, however, sent Fuller to France with an introduction to George Sand. As Charlene Avallone notes, Fuller initially regarded Sand somewhat warily as a guide for her own thinking.[16] After joining the *Tribune*, Fuller began to receive recognition as a progressive spokeswoman. Sand's work connected with her developing radical tendencies. She had read several of Sand's novels but had mixed feelings about them, finding "really shallow, and hasty" character portrayals in her work. But as she read, she felt Sand's powerful impact, pointing to the "deeply smouldering fire it burns!—Not vehement, but intense" (*Memoirs* 1:250). Sand's works invigorated Fuller's feminist drive and energized her own literary aspirations.[17] She came to see that Sand had broken through the overpowering cultural barrier that had forbidden women authors to reveal or condemn the rules that defined marriage, including the confinement and abuse that the custom often sustained. The chance to meet Sand in Paris, with Mazzini's commendation, was particularly important for her.

Nineteenth-century critics in England and America had condemned Sand's novels as lurid and dissolute. In 1839, the year when Fuller began exploring French writing, Mazzini published an extensive and erudite essay on Sand, arguing that her work was far from immoral. He praised Sand as a writer who had brought the oppression of women to light through her novels, using her life experience as her grounding. "*She* has suffered—she has revolted,—she has struggled—she has sought, hoped, found; and she has told us *all*. The long series of her compositions form a grand confession." The supposedly revealing and sensational components of Sand's work, often under attack, were for Mazzini the source of the moral power of her books. The artistic portrayal of evil is itself not evil, he contended, but instead can be, as in Sand's books, "a powerful lesson of morality." His protection of Sand illustrated what he held as a crucial principle. "The morality of a literary performance appears to us to consist far less in the choice of things represented, of topics, than in the manner in which they are treated, in the final effect which the book, by whatever means, produces on the soul."[18]

Fuller's tour of Paris was more exciting, and more mind-opening, than she could have imagined. The city was at that moment "the center of European intellectual life and a remarkable coherence characterized the thinking of its leading leftists" (SG 16). "Paris! I was sad to leave thee, thou wonderful focus," she wrote, emphasizing the city's ability to concentrate and clarify the mind. Paris "is the only school where I ever found abundance of teachers who could bear being examined by the pupil in their special branches" (SG 126). Sand was one of the most important of those teachers, even though Fuller was able to see her only briefly. Elizabeth Hoar and other friends in Concord were fascinated by the scandalous author. Fuller assured them that the stories about Sand's divorce and subsequent paramours were not "exaggerated." Indeed, "she had every reason to leave her husband—a stupid, brutal man, who insulted and neglected her." Explaining that Sand was now a respected woman, she described her as one who "takes rank in society like a man." She had recently "given her daughter in marriage," and her "son is a grown-up young man, an artist." While she made it clear to the folks at home that Sand was a woman "with high esteem" in Paris, she also acknowledged that her sexual life, by New England standards, might seem improper. "She has had a series of lovers, and I am told has one now, with whom she lives on the footing of combined means, independent friendship" (*FL* 4:256). That man was Chopin.

Fuller found in Sand a woman to respect, not only for her writing but also for the conduct of her life. She had responded to the difficult challenges she had faced, trials encountered by many women, with determination and courage, and made herself an accomplished figure. "I never shall forget her look at that moment," said Fuller, describing her introduction to Sand. "What fixed my attention was the expression of *goodness*, nobleness, and power, that pervaded the whole." Fuller recognized "the truly human heart and nature that shone in the eyes" (*Memoirs* 2:195). After an unexpectedly full afternoon of conversation, Fuller was able to have only one more brief meeting with Sand. Clearly, however, Sand had made a deep impression on her that would not be lost. "I heartily enjoyed the sense of so rich, so prolific, so ardent a genius. I liked the woman in her, too, very much; I never liked a woman better" (*Memoirs* 2:197).

Fuller's brief but intense friendship with the Polish poet Adam Mickiewicz was an even stronger influence on her during this period of emotional ferment. He believed in women's rights, a principle that was central in the teaching of Andrew Towianski, who preached mysticism and radical politics. Mickiewicz was another Parisian expatriate, a strong supporter of Mazzini and a literary romantic, familiar with Emerson's works. Fuller had been impressed after reading his lectures given at the Collège de France and went several times with the Springs to see him at the "Circle of God" meetings he conducted in Paris.[19] She reported to Emerson having "found in him the man I had long wished to see, with the intellect and passions in due proportion for a full and healthy human being, with a soul constantly inspiring" (*FL* 4:261). As Megan Marshall puts it, "she felt *recognized*" by Mickiewicz (Marshall 288). After their first meeting, Mickiewicz sent Fuller a letter that combined sincere admiration, firm advice, and a prophetic picture of her future. He recognized her as a female bearer of wisdom, but one who had not yet found her way. "Her *base*," he declared, "is in the old world; her *sphere of action* is in the new world; her *peace* is in the world to come." She would, he believed, play an important role in the coming "deliverance" of Poland, France, and America (FL 5:176).

Mickiewicz also boldly offered Fuller his advice on her virginity. Fuller's belief in virginity had been a vital component of her identity. In *Woman in the Nineteenth Century*, she had related the story of the Indian girl who "dreamt in her youth that she was betrothed to the sun." Her tribe respected her vision and allowed her to live in "a wigwam apart," in which she conducted "an independent life" (EMF 301). Mickiewicz did not criticize Fuller's virginity, but he did tell her to examine her situation as her future opened. "You have acquired the right to know and maintain the rights and obligations, the hopes and exigencies of virginity," he assured her. Nevertheless, he added, "the first step in your deliverance" was "to know if it is permitted to you to remain virgin" (FL 5:176). Permitted by whom, of course, is the obvious response of a modern reader. But Mickiewicz was not commanding Fuller. He spoke as if he recognized her as a woman able to accomplish an urgent mission. This sense of a calling had been growing in Fuller since she began her Conversations for women. Mazzini, and now Mickiewicz, were offering her not simply praise for her work but a belief that she could help to formulate "the world to come." This was, for Fuller, a source of new strength.

"I wish to be free and absolutely true to my nature"

Fuller left Paris deeply saddened by her separation from Mickiewicz. On a spring evening a month later in Rome, she exclaimed to Rebecca Spring: "Why was I not born here! Why did I ever live anywhere else!" (Capper 2:330). She had loved the art and history that Italy represented, but it was the vibrancy of the Roman streets that captured her. Rome was life in a way Fuller had never seen but had longed for. The city did much to relieve the loss of Mickiewicz, but her resentment of the Springs' insistence on a hurried exit from Paris had begun to gnaw at her. Fuller had remained in touch with Mickiewicz, regarding him as her most important adviser. But Rome was, at this moment, a new life. Part of that freshness was Giovanni Angelo Ossoli, a young man who courteously assisted her to her home on the evening of the first of April. Ossoli, age twenty-six, was the youngest son of an old and respectable but now disadvantaged family. He lived with his sister, his brother-in-law, and his ailing father (Capper 2:332). Ossoli had little education, spoke no English, and had no immediate chance for employment. But he had charm, gentleness, attentiveness, and an attractive appearance. After taking Fuller home that evening, he spent much of the next day pacing in front of her apartment in hopes of seeing her.

Fuller's initial friendship with Ossoli would last a brief two months. She was scheduled to leave Rome with the Springs in late May, traveling through northern Italy, Germany, and Switzerland and then returning to America. She would lose Italy, lose Rome, and lose Ossoli, who had proposed to her when she told him she was going home. "I loved him and felt very unhappy to leave him, but the connexion seemed so everyway unfit. I did not hesitate a moment. He, however, thought I should return to him, as I did," Fuller wrote later to her sister Ellen. "I acted upon a strong impulse. I could not analyze at all what passed in my mind" (*FL* 5:292). Although she had once yearned to travel to the land of Goethe, when she arrived in Venice she decided to break from the Springs. She returned through northern Italy alone, resuming her place as an observer and analyst of Rome and its simmering politics. She could not leave Rome after all it now meant for her—her bond with Mazzini, her obligations designated by Mickiewicz, her evening walks with Ossoli, and, deepest at this moment, Italy's intense political drama. This was, for Fuller, an alluring and worthy life, one she could not abandon.

She sent an evocative letter to the Springs the morning of April 10 to explain her surprising decision to part with them. "I was by nature destined to walk by the inner life alone," she wrote. She would make her own decisions through her innermost trust of her impulses, as she always had. "It has led, will lead me sometimes on a narrow plank across deep chasms, if I do not see it clear, if I do not balance myself exactly I must then fall and bleed and die." This, Fuller assured them, was no lark or escapade but a telling moment in life that both fixed her identity and resolved her future. "For this intellectually I am always prepared. I wish to be free and absolutely true to my nature, and if I cannot live so I do not wish to live" (*FL* 4:262–63). Searching for acknowledgment, Fuller made her letter a credo, a statement of her beliefs and her intention to live by them. Italy had become a belief, a promise that could not be broken. This was the determined grip of "self" that she had urged in the closing of *Woman in the Nineteenth Century*. Fuller's insistence that the Springs recognize her "wish to be absolutely to my nature" was the same demand that she preached in her book to the many women who aspired to live free and true to their own nature.

Sizzling just under this decision was Fuller's relationship with Mickiewicz. Observing her response to him in Paris, Rebecca Spring had asked Fuller directly if she was in love with him (Marshall 287–88). Fuller's frank reply was one of her most notable self-portrayals. "I have never sought love as a passion," she wrote. "It has always come to me as an angel bearing some good tidings." Love was welcome, she acknowledged, but she would never "detain it, or cling with a weak personality to a tie which had ceased to bind the soul" (*FL* 4:263). She moved deeply into the question of love when she confessed: "I do not know whether I have loved at all in the sense of oneness, but I have loved enough to feel the joys of presence the pangs of absence, the sweetness of hope, and the chill of disappointment. More than once my heart has bled, and my health has suffered from these things but mentally I have always found myself the gainer, always younger and more noble. I have no wish about my future course but that it should be like the past, only always more full and deeper." It is only after this admission that Fuller can respond fully to Spring's question about Mickiewicz. "He affected me like music or the richest landscape, my heart beat with joy that he at once felt beauty in me also. When I was with him I was happy; and thus far the attraction is so strong that all the way from Paris I felt as if I had left my life behind, and if I followed my inclination I should return this moment and leave Italy unseen" (*FL* 4:262–63).

Fuller's unburdening of herself through this letter certainly clarified the borders of her friendship with the Springs. It also gave her the determination to continue her stay in Italy at this climactic period of political conflict. She returned to Rome in mid-October, entering a homeland that she now considered hers. "You cannot guess how rejoiced I am!," she wrote to her mother. "The Italians sympathize with my character and understand my organization, as no other people ever did; they admire the ready eloquence of my nature, and highly prize my intelligent sympathy (such as they do not find often in foreigners) with their sufferings in the past and hopes for the future" (*FL* 4:299–300). This awareness of connection, not just with Rome but with Italy and its people, would now become a source of energy for her objective as a writer and activist. "I have not been so well since I was a child, nor so happy," she assured her mother again in a mid-December letter (*FL* 4:312). Much of this new elation she felt can be attributed to her relationship with Ossoli, but also to a political mission moving her ahead as a champion for Italy's emancipation. "I never regarded literature merely as a collection of exquisite products," she wrote, "but rather as a means of mutual interpretation" (*FL* 4:39). This task of education and mutuality stood before her as she saw Italy enter its struggle for democratic nationhood. This task of "mutual interpretation" was not fully recognized by historians until 1988, when Larry J. Reynolds noted the "organic structure" and "supple, powerful prose" of Fuller's dispatches from Italy.[20] Written with passion and purpose, Fuller's illuminating essays in the *Tribune* explained to Americans that Italy was their sister democracy.

Fuller's first Italian dispatches (her fourteenth and fifteenth, dated May and August 1847) concerned her first impressions of Rome, her travels in northern Italy, and her interest in Italian art and artists. She also developed a revulsion for the American and British tourists who seemed to puff contemptuously about what they saw. But she had her attention fixed firmly on the political atmosphere. Pope Pius IX, a priest with a liberal standing, had been elected on June 16, 1846, and all eyes in Rome were on him. In her first weeks in Rome, Fuller observed the pope intensely. She appreciated "the great moral influence" (*SG* 154) that he could deliver in Italy's hope for freedom from Austrian domination. Fuller immediately recognized "the love and expectation inspired by the present Pontiff. He is a man of noble and good aspect, who, it is easy to see, has set his heart upon doing something solid for the benefit of Man." She was aware, however, of the barriers that he faced. "How grave and sad must the Pope feel, as he sits alone and hears all this noise of expectation" (SG 136). Fuller was particularly impressed by the enormous response the Roman citizens gave to the pope when he announced reforms in the governance of the Papal States, which included Rome. "Nothing could seem more limited than this improvement but it was a great measure for Rome," she wrote. This small change brought "a torch-bearing procession" of Romans marching "as a river of fire" on the Corso to offer the pope their gratitude. "I have never seen anything finer" (SG 136–37).

This momentary flash of hope for Italian democracy would soon be dimmed, as Fuller reported in her second Italian dispatch. "At this moment there is great excitement in Italy. A supposed spy of Austria has been assassinated at Ferrara and Austrian troops are marched there." This martial seizure of a Papal State was clearly a sign of a possible attack on Rome and a potential attempt to colonize all of Italy. "The National Guard is forming. All things seem to announce that some important change is inevitable here, but what?" As she recognized, Rome was split politically. "Neither Radicals nor Moderates dare predict with confidence, and I am yet too much a stranger to speak with assurance of the impressions I have received," she told her American readers. She could only assure them that "it is impossible not to hope" (SG 146). Fuller's enchantment with Rome was closely connected to her response to the nation's birth, the growing sense of liberty among a people to whom it had been denied. Rome's rising, and the role of Pius IX as a progressive redeemer, were the dreams she had held. "Heart had spoken to heart between the Prince and the People; it was beautiful to see the immediately good influence of human feeling, generous designs, on the part of a ruler: he had wished to be a father," and the Italians had "entered at once into the relation" (SG 155).

Fuller was beginning to see, however, that "the task undertaken by the Pope seemed to present insuperable difficulties." What the Italian people needed could not be given to them by the pontiff. It would take other leaders with other measures to bring Italy together and make it a democracy. "Our age is one where all things tend to a great crisis," she wrote, "not merely to revolution but to radical reform" (SG 155). In a forceful declaration, she insisted that Rome's people must arrive at a new vision of their history and their future. "From the people themselves the help must come, and not from princes: in the new state of things there will be none but natural princes, great men. From the aspirations of the general heart, from the teachings of conscience in individuals, and not from an old ivy-covered church, long since undermined, corroded by Time and gnawed by vermin, the help must come. Rome, to resume her glory, must cease to be an ecclesiastical Capital" (SG 156).

"This cause is OURS"

Writing to Emerson in late December of 1847, Fuller explained her confidence in Pius IX. "He is a real great heart, a generous man. The love for him is genuine, and I like to be within its influence. It was his heart that gave the impulse, and this people has shown, to the shame of English and other prejudice, how unspoiled they were at the core, how open, nay, how wondrous swift to answer a generous appeal!" (FL 4:315). The same month she had also received an extensive letter from Mazzini, who had been traveling for the past two months in Switzerland and France before returning to London. Barred from Italy, he had been measuring the heat among his friends and associates as Europe moved toward insurgence. Mazzini spoke directly to Fuller about the growing campaign for a democratic and unified Italy. "Our people want truth, and they shall know it," he assured her. Mazzini, however, had some doubts about the pope as a political leader and feared that governance of Rome or all of Italy from the papacy would be disastrous. "Pius IX is evidently a good *man*: a charitable Christian," he wrote, "but as a king he has neither genius nor energy." He believed that the "Papacy and Austria" were "the two great enemies" of Italy's drives for unity and independence and would eventually fall. Cautioning Fuller against expectations of revolution immediately, he advised her to "let a few months pass" as Italy's attitude developed. "All you see is the mere ebullition preceding the true creative crisis."[21]

Despite Mazzini's uncertainty, Fuller had been thrilled by an earlier visit to Florence in which crowds gathered to celebrate the pope's establishment of the National Guard, a forward-facing action that was "hailed" by the Italians as "the first step toward truly national institutions and a representation of the people." Fuller was impressed by "that beautiful poetic manner peculiar to this artist people" and enthralled by "the spirit, so great and tender, that melts my heart to think of." This was, for her, "the spirit of true religion—such, my Country." She saw in this moment in Florence what the first American patriots had seen: "that all men have equal rights, and that these are *birth*-rights, derived from God alone" (SG 158–59). This stirring transfer of principled thought, sent from Italy back to America, is one of Fuller's most radiant avowals of her spiritual patriotism. She envisions a fragmented Italy becoming a new European America—a nation whose birth would also bring the slavery-polluted United States to its purification. "I earnestly hope [for] some expression of sympathy from my country toward Italy," she wrote. "This cause is OURS, above all others; we ought to show that we feel it to be so," she insisted. "In many ways she is of kin to us; she is the country of Columbus, of Amerigo, of Cabot.... Ah! America" (SG 160–61).

Fuller continued to express her disappointment with America's failures in a dispatch for New Year's Day of 1848, "a few New-Year's reflections" for her readers (SG 161). These "reflections" were among her most disparaging assaults on America's failure to live up to its democratic responsibilities, and they also express her own acknowledgment of "this horrible cancer of Slavery" and the millstone it had proved to be around the neck of her country (SG 165). Here Fuller moved beyond the bonds between America and Italy and searched "the history of our planet" only to see "a crashing of the mass of men beneath the feet of a few." She was moved to ask, "Where is the genuine Democracy to which the rights of all men are holy?" (SG 163). Europe, as she had seen it, had not yet satisfied her strong drive to find a form of social life in which all individuals have the opportunity to develop the soul within them. What she had found in Europe had been "this hollow England, with its monstrous wealth and cruel poverty," and "this poor

France, so full of talent, so adroit, yet so shallow and glossy still." She sighed over "this Italy bound down by treacherous hands in all the force of genius," but her deepest condemnation was the question she posed to "thou, my country! will thou not be more true?" It was America's responsibility, as Fuller insisted, to give Italy the support that America had once been given, "a new world, a new chance" (SG 164).

What held America back, as Fuller had now come to see clearly, was the problem of slavery. "How it pleases me here to think of the Abolitionists!" With that exclamation, she offered both a condemnation of American slavery and a tribute to those who were contending against it. Here she confessed her own failure to recognize more deeply the importance of the abolitionist cause. "I could never endure to be with them at home, they were so tedious, often so narrow, always so rabid and exaggerated in their tone," she admitted. "But, after all, they had a high motive, something eternal in their desire and life" (SG 166). She told her readers, with blistering intensity, that they had not met their obligation. "Yet, oh Eagle," she cried out to America, "thou wert to be the advance-guard of Humanity, the herald of all Progress; how often hast thou betrayed this high commission!" (SG 164). Italy's struggle for its independence had become a mirror of America's struggle for an egalitarian society. It was the same fight. Looking at America's hideous oppression of the slaves and its "wicked War" with Mexico to protect slave owner interests, she found herself incapable of preaching democracy in Europe. "How dare I speak of these things here? I listen to the same arguments against the emancipation of Italy, that are used against the emancipation of our blacks." America is "the darkest offender, because with the least excuse" (SG 165).

"His love for me has been unswerving and most tender"

Well into December, a period in which Fuller had written a remarkable series of reports on Rome, she struck a barrier that threatened her future. She recognized that she was pregnant. Her letters to Emerson on December 20 and the recently married Caroline Sturgis Tappan on January 11 suggest her emotional condition. "Soon I must begin to exert myself," she told Emerson, "for there is this incubus of the future, and none to help me, if I am not prudent to face it. So ridiculous, too, this mortal coil,—such small things!" She even seemed to feel that her days in her beloved Italy were over. "Had I only come ten years earlier! Now my life must be a failure" (FL 4:315). She also appeared upset in her letter to Caroline. "When I arrived in Rome, I was at first intoxicated to be here. The weather was beautiful, and many circumstances combined to place me in a kind of passive, childlike well-being. That is all over now, and, at present, see no way out, except through the gate of death." Her letters did not openly tell of her pregnancy, calling her condition "all a dark, sad enigma" (FL 5:43), but her hopelessness suggested her acute misery. Adding to her woes were Rome's torrential rains. "To return to Rome: what a Rome!—the fortieth day of rain, and damp, and abominable reeking odors.... It has been dark all day, though the lamp has only been lit half an hour" (SG 203). Gradually, however, Fuller was able to escape this desperation, principally with the help and support of Ossoli. They were not married when Fuller realized she was pregnant, and she was unsure how he would react to her condition. As she would later write to her mother, "His love for me has been unswerving and most tender," and he had augmented that with "sweet domestic graces" and "excellent practical sense" (FL 5:261). All these gifts would prove essential in the coming months, as their child was brought into the world in good health. In the meantime, the secrecy surrounding the pregnancy and the birth was crucial for both. Ossoli's family, having long connections with papal offices, would surely disapprove, and he would lose his place in the Civic Guard, his only occupation. Fuller's reputation as an author and journalist would also be endangered if news of her situation were to spread. To avoid revealing their out-of-wedlock pregnancy, they also decided to marry secretly.[22]

In late May, Fuller and Ossoli left Rome together to find an undisclosed and secure place where she could continue her pregnancy without the risk of discovery. This would, however, mean long periods of separation because of Ossoli's duties. With his help, Fuller moved to the remote mountain village of L'Aquila in May of 1848, and then in July to Rieti, somewhat closer to Rome. The separation was emotionally painful for her, and problematic for her efforts to keep watch over developments in Rome's politics. As she soon wrote to Ossoli: "Now for two weeks I have not received any papers, nor have I heard from you in reply to my last two letters. I know nothing about the things that I am interested in; I feel lonely, imprisoned, too unhappy" (*FL* 5:78). Fuller's hunger for information—written and spoken—was voracious.

Ossoli seems to have gotten the message. As Joan von Mehren notes, he now "kept her well informed" with newspapers and reports of the current political discussions (von Mehren 285). Angelo Eugene Philip Ossoli, who came to be known as Nino, was born on September 5, 1848. His father was able to be there for the birth and arranged for his baptism, after some discussion with Fuller, two months later on November 5 (Capper 2:397–400). After the birth and convalescence, Fuller realized that she must return to her writing and restore her bond with Rome. To bring Nino, however, would endanger Ossoli's relations with his family, his place in the guard, and her reputation in Rome. As Hudspeth writes, "Fuller had to balance her love for the baby against the necessity to leave him and return to Rome" (*FL* 5:10–11). Knowing that she must resume her reports for the *Tribune* and move forward with her book, Fuller and Ossoli left Nino in the care of the local family who had been tending him. With Ossoli's help, Fuller returned to Rome in early November (Capper 2:395–401, Marshall 322–33).

The months of Fuller's pregnancy occurred during a politically decisive period in Italy's history. Her dispatches of late 1847 and early 1848 are among her most insightful works, and they reveal a building militancy in her thinking. In her New Year's Day dispatch, she noted her concern that the pope had begun to step back from the political helm in Rome. While his hesitation did not "weaken my personal feelings toward this excellent man," she wrote, "I am only disappointed that his good heart has not carried him on a little farther" (*SG* 199). By early spring her patience with him had apparently vanished amid the eruptions of insurgency in Italy. "There is news that the revolution has now broken out in Naples" and "aggressions on the part of Austrians continue in the North," she wrote in late January (*SG* 208). In March she applauded "the victorious resistance of Sicily and the revolution of Naples" (SG 210). Fuller had made herself a citizen of Rome when she returned and had now become a rabid Italian partisan. Her fervor became more ardent due to the situation in France. "The news of the dethronement of Louis Philippe reached us just after the close of the Carnival. It was just a year from my leaving Paris. I did not think, as I looked with such disgust on the empire of sham he had established in France, and saw the soul of the people imprisoned and held fast as an iron vice, that it would burst its chains so soon" (SG 211). This crisis, she knew, would have compelling implications throughout Europe.

Fuller's response was noteworthy, a mark of the radical political standpoint she had reached during her European travels. "France has done gloriously," she wrote, though the recent news "sounds ominous." Even so, "it is well; whatever blood is to be shed, whatever altars cast down, those tremendous problems MUST be solved, whatever the cost!" This was, she also believed, not only a rebirth for Europe but a crucial lesson for the United States as well. The people of America "may learn the real meaning of the words FRATERNITY, EQUALITY" and "the needs of a true Democracy." Most importantly, Americans may "learn to guard, the true aristocracy of a nation, the only really noble—the LABORING CLASSES" (SG 211). She offered a series of positive signs of the reshaping of Europe: the defeat of Metternich in Austria and the successful battles of Milan and Venice, among others. In Rome, she wrote, these events brought an "indescribable rapture" as the people began to believe that freedom was near (SG 212). In late April, however, the Romans sustained an enormous disappointment when the pope backed away from any support or command of a new republic. "The loss of Pius IX. is for the moment a great one," Fuller commented. "His name had real moral weight; was a trumpet appeal to sentiment. It is not the same with any man that is left. There is not one that can be truly a leader in the Roman Dominion, not one who has even great intellectual weight" (SG 229). Fuller's distress was grave, but her devotion to Rome was not lost. She would stay with her Italian companions. "I remain at present here," she vowed. "Should my hopes be dashed to the ground, it will not change my faith, but the struggle for its manifestation is to me of vital interest" (SG 230).

As the insurrection in Italy grew, Fuller became more passionate in her dedication to Rome and more dismayed by American politics. "My friends write to urge my return; they talk of our country as the land of the Future." But the "spirit" that once gave America its greatness she now found in Rome. "My country is at present spoiled by prosperity, stupid with the lust of gain, soiled by crime in its willing perpetuation of Slavery, shamed by an unjust war, noble sentiment much forgotten even by individuals, the aims of politicians selfish or petty, the literature frivolous and venal." She saw in the present no signs of the egalitarian principles that had brought America to its prominence. "She is not dead, but in my time she sleepeth, and the spirit of our fathers flames no more, but lies hid beneath the ashes" (SG 230).

Fuller's early 1848 dispatches were grounded in the hope that true democracies would return and eventually become the governing systems of Europe. Italy, she hoped, would set the example for this new nation. When she returned from Rieti to Rome in early November, her hopes seemed shattered when Italy's most dramatic political event yet occurred. Pius IX, having backed away from the governing of Rome and other papal locations, had chosen Count Pellegrino Rossi, an expert in law and administration, as his closest adviser. Rossi's resistance to political reform, however, had inflamed many of the progressives of Rome. Rossi was assassinated at the Palazzo della Cancelleria on November 15, 1848, a stunning incident that exposed a rising displeasure toward the pope. As the anger continued to intensify among the militant populace, the pope escaped from Rome in disguise to find protection in Gaeta, leaving the people of Rome to build a new government. Fuller, who had witnessed these events, was exultant.

Reform was burning among the Romans, she believed, and would bring "great dramatic interest historically—of bearing infinitely important ideally" (SG 231). By "ideally" she meant the practice of the ideas and principles that would carry Rome to its status as a democracy.

Fuller stood unbending in her belief in the self-governing principles that Italy's people had adopted. She herself had embraced the city for its people's peacefulness and tranquility. "City of the Soul! yes it is *that*; the very dust magnetizes you, and thousand spells have been chaining you in every careless, every murmuring moment." It was for her, in the deepest way, the place of "repose." "For whatever be the revolutions, tumults, panics, hopes of the present day, still the temper of life here is Repose" (SG 238). When the disguised pope escaped after the Rossi assassination, "Rome remained quite cool and composed" (SG 244). Even so, Fuller recognized the momentous nature of Rome's uprising. In one of her most splendid passages, she explained that "the revolution, like all genuine ones, has been instinctive, its results unexpected and surprising to the greater part of those who achieved them. The waters that had flowed so secretly beneath the crust of habit that many never heard their murmur, unless in dreams, have suddenly burst to light in full and beautiful jets; all rush to drink the pure and living draught" (SG 250). She was stirred with the development of the democratic Rome, finding a particular pleasure in the moment when an "immense crowd of people surrounded the *Palazzo della Cancelleria*" and waited until "one o'clock in the morning of the 9th February" to witness the "proclamation of the Republic" (SG 256). This exultant civic pride, something she had not seen elsewhere in Europe or America, fueled her creative and historical resources. "Of all this great drama I have much to write," she said. "The materials are over-rich" (SG 237).

"Should I never return"

Behind the uprising in Rome, troubling events were emerging, and as Marshall notes, "By the time that she returned to the city, nearly all of Europe's revolutions had failed or lost their momentum" (Marshall 329). This Europe-wide antebellum eventually left Rome in the hands of France, which responded to the pope's call to restore him to the Vatican. French troops landed near Rome on April 25, 1849, with immense advantages in both soldiers and cannon. At Mazzini's call, Giuseppe Garibaldi, a military prodigy and democratically minded Italian patriot, took charge of the troops defending Rome. After a long and brutal siege by the French, one that appeared to be moving toward a slaughter, Garibaldi's troops battled through the French lines, escaping from Rome.[23] The city was finally occupied by the French on July 3. The Roman Republic had been abolished.

Both Fuller and Ossoli had joined the Romans who battled desperately for the salvation of the new republic. Fuller was called into service by an Italian friend, Princess Cristina Trivulzio di Belgioioso, to help administer the hospitals for the injured soldiers. The princess "was born of one of the noblest families of the Milanese" and was a woman of literary talents with interests "in the Socialist direction" (SG 281). Her faith in Fuller, and her support, were crucial in this task. Fuller's duties were of the most urgent and distressing kind: the treatment of severe wounds and the consoling of soldiers approaching death. These responsibilities multiplied, of course, as the bombardments continued (Capper 2:448–58). Ossoli, as a member of the Civic Guard, was in the heat of the battle, narrowly missing injury or death from the violent gunfire and cannon shot.

Fuller sent a letter to Emerson on June 10, a touching document which attested to her anxieties. "I received your letter amid the round of cannonade and musketry," she told him. "It was a terrible battle fought here from the first till the last light of day. I could see all its progress from my balcony. The Italians fought like lions. It is a truly heroic spirit that animates them." The opening of her letter, with its drama and its terror, called for both his understanding and his acceptance. "I go almost daily to the hospitals," she told him, "and, though I have suffered,—for I had no idea before, how terrible gunshot-wounds and wound-fever are," she had "taken pleasure, and great pleasure," she emphasized, "in being with the men," all of whom were "moved with a noble spirit." These words, spoken to a close friend who had urged her strongly to leave Italy, emphasized the intensity of her fight for the principles. She made it clear that the battle was a bitter one. "The palace of the Pope," she told him, "is now used for the convalescents," and "I walk with them," she said, "one with his sling, another with his crutch" (FL 5:239).

Midway through the letter Fuller turned the justification of her compassionate work into a stunning plea for Emerson's understanding. She implored him to recognize that she had given herself to the truth as she had seen it. "Should I never return," we almost hear her sigh, and "sometimes I despair of doing so, it seems so far off, so difficult. I am caught in such a net of ties here,—if ever you know of my life here, I think you will only wonder at the constancy with which I have sustained myself." She had not walked thoughtlessly into a dangerous ambush, she argued. Her eyes had been open to the consequences of her decisions. She had in many ways benefited from the "observation" of life in Italy, the work that had sustained her so far. But the destruction of the Roman Republic, which she now saw as inevitable, marked a world she had now lost. "Meanwhile," she asked of Emerson, "love me all you can; let me feel, that, amid the fearful agitations of the world, there are pure hands, with healthful, even pulse, stretched out toward me, if I claim their grasp" (*FL* 5:240). She closed her letter with a frank, and forsaken, confession. "I know not, dear friend, whether I ever shall get home across that great ocean, but here in Rome I shall no longer wish to live. O, Rome, *my* country! could I imagine that the triumph of what I held dear was to heap such desolation on thy head!" (*FL* 5: 240). Fuller's inconsolable letter is the clearest indication of her veiled despair as Rome gradually came to its end. Rome was no longer hers. The French occupation of the city produced a swift restoration of an obdurate papal rule, and it became quite dangerous for the those who supported the republic. Fuller needed to find a place of recovery and familial repose. As she wrote on July 10 in one of her last dispatches: "I am sick of breathing the same air with men capable of a part so utterly cruel and false. As soon as I can I shall take refuge in the mountains, if it be possible to find an obscure nook unpervaded by these convulsions. Let not my friends be surprised if they do not hear from me for some time. I may not feel like writing. I have seen too much sorrow, and alas! without power to aid" (*SG* 308). After helping a stunned and bewildered Mazzini make his way back to London, Fuller and Ossoli left Rome on July 12, finding comfort in Florence.

"Here lie my hopes now"

In Fuller's late dispatches, as warfare approached and broke out, we find some of her most evocative and revelatory assertions about democracy and its future. Larry Reynolds observes that through her experiences in Europe, she had "assumed the role of a prophetess."[24] She recognized Rome's defeat as a first step toward freedom. Writing as the French siege began, she declared that "the struggle is now fairly, thoroughly commenced between the principle of Democracy and the old powers, no longer legitimate. That struggle may last fifty years, and the earth be watered with blood and tears of more than one generation, but the result is sure." Having watched the uprisings of peoples all over Italy, she perceived a newfound energy that was invincible. "*The work is done*; the revolution in Italy is now radical," she asserted, "nor can it stop till Italy become independent and united as a republic" (SG 277–78). As Barbara Packer writes, "Fuller's faith in the ultimate direction of the historical process sustained her even during the last awful days of the bombardment of Rome and the collapse of the Republic."[25] This prophetic radicalism looked to the people themselves as the one force that could instigate a governance of equality and freedom.

After Rome fell, Fuller decided to go back to America. She realized, with sadness, that Rome was no longer her home. Her husband and child gave her a strong reason to return. She recognized her mother's deep love, and Greeley was surely waiting for more of her well-informed writing in New York. Even so, there were impediments to her return to America. As Capper notes, "Ocean voyages had long frightened her" (Capper 2:500). After considerable searching, Fuller chose a small ship, the *Elizabeth*, for the journey to America. The ship departed on May 17, 1850. In July, after a long voyage, a storm near Fire Island in New York wrecked the ship, killing Fuller, her husband, her child, and many others who were aboard. This tragic death is heartrending when we think deeply of how she brought so much to America.

"Here lie my hopes now," she wrote in a last closing dispatch. "I believed before I came to Europe in what is called Socialism, as the inevitable sequence to the tendencies and wants of the era, but I did not think these vast changes in modes of government, education and daily life, would be effected as rapidly as I now think they will, because they must. The world can no longer stand without them" (SG 320). In the first outbursts of the European insurgencies and the woeful downfall of the Roman revolt, Fuller saw inevitable victory rather than a decisive defeat. The world, she recognized, was in transformation. "The next revolution, here and elsewhere, will be radical," she avowed. "It will be an uncompromising revolution" (SG 321).

Fuller believed that destroyed Rome would become its own democracy, in its own way. As she sailed for America, she knew that she had imprinted her values on the nation that was moving toward a battle for the truth. Fuller had expressed in her letters and journalism the truths she had learned through her relationships and life experiences in Europe. Many women had been able to find their inner strength through reading Fuller or hearing her voice. As she declared in her late dispatches, the struggle for democracy "may last fifty years, and the earth be watered with blood and tears of more than one generation, but the result is sure" (SG 278). Fuller's voice was influential for antislavery radicals such as Julia Ward Howe and Thomas Wentworth Higginson, both Fuller biographers. They saw Fuller as a key figure in the "New Era" of progressive American politics (RV 50–55).[26] They saw Fuller's principles as guides to the battle for the end of slavery, the crucial step in the maturing of the American nation. Fuller's voice stayed with them. It endures now with us.

NOTES

Chapter 1

1 *The Collected Works of Ralph Waldo Emerson*, ed. Alfred R. Ferguson et al., 10 vols. (Cambridge, MA: Belknap Press of Harvard University Press, 1971–2013), 1:13. Cited as *CW*.
2 *Memoirs of Margaret Fuller Ossoli*, ed. Ralph Waldo Emerson, William Henry Channing, and James Freeman Clarke, 2 vols. (Boston: Phillips, Sampson and Company, 1852), 1:114. Cited as *Memoirs*.
3 *The Letters of Margaret Fuller*, ed. Robert N. Hudspeth, 6 vols. (Ithaca, NY: Cornell University Press, 1983–1994), 6:170. Cited as *FL*.
4 For reassessments of the transcendentalist movement that give Fuller due attention, see Barbara Packer, *The Transcendentalists* (Athens: University of Georgia Press, 2007); and Philip F. Gura, *American Transcendentalism: A History* (New York: Hill and Wang, 2007). Joel Myerson's anthology *Transcendentalism: A Reader* (New York: Oxford University Press, 2000) includes extensive selections from Fuller's work. For critical interest in Fuller, see Larry J. Reynolds, "Prospects for the Study of Margaret Fuller," *Resources for American Literary Study* 26 (2000): 139–58.
5 *William Ellery Channing: Selected Writings*, ed. David M. Robinson (New York: Paulist Press, 1985), 145–65.
6 James Freeman Clarke, *Autobiography, Diary, and Correspondence*, ed. Edward Everett Hale (Boston: Houghton Mifflin, 1891), 39. Cited as JFC.
7 For a discussion of Hartley's work, see Barbara Bowen Oberg, "David Hartley and the Association of Ideas," *Journal of the History of Ideas* 37, no. 3 (July–September 1976): 441–54.

8 James Marsh's 1829 edition of Coleridge's *Aids to Reflection* was one of the most important acts of literary transmission in the early nineteenth century. Marsh made the work newly available in New England and provided an explanatory introduction that was perhaps as influential as Coleridge's text itself.
9 S. T. Coleridge, *Aids to Reflection*, 1st American ed. from the 1st London ed., with a preliminary essay and additional notes by James Marsh (Burlington, VT: Chauncy Goodrich, 1829), 141, 145. See also Peter Carafiol's discussion of Marsh's edition, which provided an explanatory introduction that was important to the impact of Coleridge's text. Peter Carafiol, *Transcendent Reason: James Marsh and the Forms of Romantic Thought* (Tallahassee: University Presses of Florida, 1982).
10 *The Journals and Miscellaneous Notebooks of Ralph Waldo Emerson*, ed. William H. Gilman et al., 16 vols. (Cambridge, MA: Belknap Press of Harvard University Press, 1960–1982), 5:273. Cited as *JMN*.
11 Frederic Henry Hedge, "Coleridge's Literary Character," *Christian Examiner* 14 (March 1833): 109–29.
12 *The Letters of James Freeman Clarke to Margaret Fuller*, ed. John Wesley Thomas (Hamburg: Cram, de Gruyter & Co., 1957), 20. Cited as *JFC Fuller*.
13 Samuel Taylor Coleridge, *The Friend: A Series of Essays*, 3 vols. (London: Rest Fenner, 1818), 3:22.
14 Thomas Carlyle, "Novalis," *The Foreign Review* 4, no. 7 (1829): 97–141, http://novalis.autorenverzeichnis.de/carlyle/3.html. Cited as CNovalis.
15 Barbara L. Packer, *The Transcendentalists* (Athens: University of Georgia Press, 2007), 32.
16 *The Essential Margaret Fuller*, ed. Jeffrey Steele (New Brunswick, NJ: Rutgers University Press, 1992), 38. Cited as *EMF*.
17 Elizabeth Ware Rotch Farrar was born in Europe to American parents. Raised a Quaker, she later converted to Unitarianism. She married the Harvard mathematician and astronomer John Farrar in 1828 and was a well-liked and prominent hostess for conversations and lectures. She brought together many men and women with literary and artistic interests. She became a mentor to Fuller and introduced her to several people who would have a large place in Fuller's life, including Samuel Gray Ward, Elizabeth Barker, Harriet Martineau, and Emerson. For discussions of her life and achievements, see Elizabeth Bancroft Schlesinger, "Two Early Harvard Wives: Eliza Farrar and Eliza Follen, *New England Quarterly* 38 (June 1965): 147–67; Schlesinger, "Eliza Ware Rotch Farrar," in *Notable American Women, 1607–1950: A Biographical Dictionary*, ed. Edward T. James, Janet Wilson James, and Paul S. Boyer, 3 vols. (Cambridge, MA: Belknap Press of Harvard University Press, 1971), 1:601–2; and Farrar's memoir *Recollections of Seventy Years* (Boston: Ticknor and Fields, 1865).
18 Thomas Wentworth Higginson, *Margaret Fuller Ossoli* (Boston: Houghton, Mifflin, 1899), 35. Cited as Higginson.
19 Joan von Mehren, *Minerva and the Muse: A Life of Margaret Fuller* (Amherst: University of Massachusetts Press, 1994), 35. Cited as von Mehren.

20 Mrs. John Farrar, *The Young Lady's Friend* (1836; New York: Samuel S. & William Wood. Parker, 1845), 2.
21 Charles Capper, *Margaret Fuller: An American Romantic Life*, vol. 1, *The Private Years* (New York: Oxford University Press, 1992), 10–12. Cited as Capper 1.
22 Paula Blanchard, *Margaret Fuller: From Transcendentalism to Revolution* (New York: Delacorte Press, 1978), 93.
23 See Charles Capper, *Margaret Fuller: An American Romantic Life*, vol. 2, *The Public Years* (New York: Oxford University Press, 2007), 47–48. Cited as Capper 2. Capper connects "Autobiographical Romance" with other stories Fuller was writing at that time for *The Dial*, noting that it was "not fulfilling that goal" (47).
24 Sidonie Smith, "Resisting the Gaze of Embodiment: Women's Autobiography in the Nineteenth Century," in *American Women's Autobiography: Fea(s)ts of Memory*, ed. Margo Culley (Madison: University of Wisconsin Press, 1992), 85, 84.
25 Megan Marshall, *Margaret Fuller: A New American Life* (Boston: Houghton Mifflin Harcourt, 2013), 6. Cited as Marshall.
26 For readings of the "transparent eye-ball" passage, see Jonathan Bishop, *Emerson on the Soul* (Cambridge, MA: Harvard University Press, 1964), 9–15; Merton M. Sealts Jr., *Emerson on the Scholar* (Columbia: University of Missouri Press, 1992), 67–73; Laura Dassow Walls, *Emerson's Life in Science: The Culture of Truth* (Ithaca, NY: Cornell University Press, 2003), 98–101; David M. Robinson, "Partakers of the Divine Nature: Ripley's Discourses and the Transcendental Annus Mirabilis," *Religions* 9, no. 21 (2018): 12, https://doi.org/10.3390/rel9010012; David Greenham, *Emerson's Transatlantic Romanticism* (New York: Palgrave Macmillan, 2012). The publication of a manuscript cartoon of a barefoot eyeball in top hat and tails by Emerson's friend and disciple Christopher Pearse Cranch, a poet and landscape painter, boosted the fame of Emerson's metaphor. See F. DeWolfe Miller, *Christopher Pearse Cranch and His Caricatures of New England Transcendentalism* (Cambridge, MA: Harvard University Press, 1951).
27 For an illuminating discussion of Fuller's use of Greek mythology, see Andrew P. White, "'Expanding in the Sun': Margaret Fuller's 'Autobiographical Romance' and the Hellenic Topography of Early American Feminism," in *Anglo-American Perceptions of Hellenism*, ed. Tatiani Rapatzikou (Newcastle upon Tyne, UK: Cambridge Scholars Publishing, 2007), 116–28.

Chapter 2

1 Christina Zwarg, *Feminist Conversations: Fuller, Emerson, and the Play of Reading* (Ithaca, NY: Cornell University Press, 1995), 6. Cited as Zwarg.
2 Zwarg 67. Fuller would eventually publish two excerpts of her translation of *Tasso* in the January 1842 *Dial*. The complete translation was published posthumously in Margaret Fuller, *Art, Literature, and the Drama* (Boston: Brown, Taggard, and Chase, 1860), 1–449, a volume edited by her brother Arthur B. Fuller. On Fuller's

composition of this translation and her readings in German literature at Groton, see Capper 1:128–31.

3 See Margaret Fuller's review of Richard Henry Wilde, *Conjectures and Researches concerning the Love, Madness, and Imprisonment of Torquato Tasso, Dial* 2, no. 1 (January 1842): 399–407, quotations 400.

4 See Marshall 91–92.

5 See Capper 1:155, 163–65.

6 See Capper 1:165 on Fuller's financial situation and the cost of the trip with the Farrars.

7 See Robert Hudspeth's description of the manuscript, "May not be a letter, for the manuscript is not creased" (*FL* 1:242).

8 Margaret Fuller, "Present State of German Literature," *American Monthly Magazine* 8 (July 1836): 1–13, American Periodicals Series Online. Cited as MF Pres. Fuller frames her essay as a review of G. W. Haven's recent translation of Heinrich Heine's *History of Modern Polite Literature in Germany* (1836). See Capper 1:175–80 for further details on its context.

9 See Perry Miller, ed., *The Transcendentalists: An Anthology* (Cambridge, MA: Harvard University Press, 1950), 106–56.

10 Zwarg's revisionist account of the depth and intellectual importance of the Fuller-Emerson friendship in *Feminist Conversations* remains an indispensable account of this complex and much-discussed relationship and did much to bring Fuller more centrally into literary and feminist studies.

11 On Fuller's meeting Emerson, and on the long foreground that preceded it, see Capper 1:184–90.

12 For Fuller's "Translator's Preface," see S. M. Fuller, *Conversations with Goethe in the Last Years of his Life, Translated from the German of Eckermann* (Boston: Hilliard, Gray, and Company, 1839). Cited *MFE*.

13 For an informative discussion of the Daimonic, see Joseph C. Schöpp, "Playing the Eclectic: Margaret Fuller's Creative Appropriation of Goethe," in *Margaret Fuller: Transatlantic Crossings in a Revolutionary Age*, ed. Charles Capper and Cristina Giorcelli (Madison: University of Wisconsin Press, 2007), 27–44.

14 See Megan Marshall, "Margaret Fuller on Music's 'Everlasting Yes': A Romantic Critic in the Romantic Era," in *Margaret Fuller and Her Circles*, ed. Brigitte Bailey, Katheryn P. Viens, and Conrad Edick Wright (Durham: University of New Hampshire Press, 2013), 148–60.

15 I capitalize Conversations in referring to these formal public events to distinguish them from ordinary conversations. Description and analysis of Fuller's Conversations are immense. See Bell Gale Chevigny, *The Woman and the Myth: Margaret Fuller's Life and Writings* (1976), rev. ed. (Boston: Northeastern University Press, 1994), 224–28, cited as Chevigny; Zwarg 163–67 and 255–57; von Mehren 114–19; Capper 1:290–306; Sandra M. Gustafson, "Choosing a Medium: Margaret Fuller and the Forms of Sentiment," *American Quarterly* 47, no. 1 (March 1995): 34–65; Mary E. Kelley, *Learning to Stand and Speak: Women, Education, and Public Life in*

America's Republic (Chapel Hill: University of North Carolina Press, 2006), cited as Kelley; Marshall 132–41.
16 Robert Hudspeth notes that Fuller was "thoroughly familiar" with the works of de Staël (*FL* 6:183n9). On de Staël's influence on Fuller, see Kelley, 233–35.
17 Ellen, Moers, *Literary Women* (Garden City, NY: Doubleday, 1976), 173–200, quotations 184, 185.
18 See Marshall 132–41 and von Mehren 114–19 for informative descriptions of the Conversations.
19 For Alcott's role in Fuller's move to the Greene Street School, see Capper 1:204–5. For a valuable analysis of the impact of Fuller's teaching experience on the development of her Conversations, see Derek Pacheco, *Moral Enterprise: Literature and Education in Antebellum America* (Columbus: Ohio State University Press, 2013), 105–18. For the documents connected with Fuller's teaching, see Frank Shuffleton, "Margaret Fuller at the Greene Street School: The Journal of Evelina Metcalf," in *Studies in the American Renaissance, 1985*, ed. Joel Myerson (Charlottesville: University Press of Virginia, 1985), 29–46; Laraine R. Fergenson, "Margaret Fuller as a Teacher in Providence: The School Journal of Ann Brown," in *Studies in the American Renaissance, 1991*, ed. Joel Myerson (Charlottesville: University Press of Virginia, 1991), 59–118; Paula Kopacz, "The School Journal of Hannah (Anna) Gale," in *Studies in the American Renaissance, 1996*, ed. Joel Myerson (Charlottesville: University Press of Virginia, 1996), 67–113; Daniel Shealey, "Margaret Fuller and Her 'Maiden': Evelina Metcalf's 1838 School Journal," in Myerson, *Studies in the American Renaissance, 1996*, 41–65; and Granville Ganter and Hani Sarij, "'May We Put Forth Our Leaves': Rhetoric in the School Journal of Mary Ware Allen, Student of Margaret Fuller, 1837–38," *Proceedings of the American Antiquarian Society* 117 (2007): 61–142.
20 Amanda Ritchie, "Margaret Fuller's First Conversation Series: A Discovery in the Archives," *Legacy: A Journal of American Women Writers* 18, no. 2 (2001): 216–31. Cited as Ritchie. As Ritchie notes, these gatherings were much smaller than the ones Fuller launched in the fall and included the noted painter Washington Allston and Harvard's leading linguist, George Ticknor, who had himself translated, but not published, Goethe's immensely popular first novel, *The Sorrows of Young Werther*. As Ritchie shows (218–19), Fuller looked on these more focused and more intimate conversations as rehearsals for the larger project of the Conversations, which she had already begun to plan.
21 See Zwarg 163–67; Capper 1:252–306; and Marshall 132–41 for helpful accounts of the Conversations and their importance. For Elizabeth Palmer Peabody's transcript of the first Conversation, see Nancy Craig Simmons, "Margaret Fuller's Boston Conversations: The 1839–1840 Series," in *Studies in the American Renaissance, 1994*, ed. Joel Myerson (Charlottesville: University Press of Virginia, 1994), 195–226. Cited as Simmons. For Caroline Healey Dall's recollection of the last Conversation, see Caroline Healey Dall, ed., *Margaret and Her Friends* (1895; rpt. New York: Arno, 1972); and Joel Myerson, "Mrs. Dall Edits Miss Fuller: The

Story of *Margaret and Her Friends*," *Papers of the Bibliographical Society of America* 72 (1978): 187–200. See *FL* 2:86–89 for Fuller's letter to Sophia Ripley on her plans for the Conversations.

22 As Simmons writes, Peabody worked "from notes (or 'abstracts') rather than unaided memory" and "reconstructed" one of the sessions that she missed "from another woman's verbal account" (Simmons 198). She seems to have recognized the historical importance of the lectures, as did Elizabeth Hoar, copyist of the manuscript that is now extant at the American Antiquarian Society, Worcester, MA. Emerson's account of Fuller's Conversations in *Memoirs* 1 (329–31) is based on Peabody's account.

23 See Phyllis Cole, "Woman Questions: Emerson, Fuller, and New England Reform," in *Transient and Permanent: The Transcendentalist Movement and Its Contexts*, ed. Charles Capper and Conrad E. Wright (Boston: Massachusetts Historical Society and Northeastern University Press, 1999), 408–46.

24 *The Early Lectures of Ralph Waldo Emerson*, ed. Stephen E. Whicher et al., 3 vols. (Cambridge, MA: Belknap Press of Harvard University Press, 1966–1972), 3:256. Cited as *EEL*.

25 See Phyllis Cole, "The Nineteenth-Century Women's Rights Movement and the Canonization of Margaret Fuller," *ESQ: A Journal of the American Renaissance* 27 (1998): 1–28; and Cole, "Stanton, Fuller, and the Grammar of Romanticism," *New England Quarterly* 73 (2000): 33–59.

26 John S. Dwight, ed., *Select Minor Poems: Translated from the German of Goethe and Schiller. With Notes* (Boston: Hilliard, Gray, and Company, 1839).

27 See Ora Frishberg Saloman, *Beethoven's Symphonies and J. S. Dwight: The Birth of American Music Criticism* (Boston: Northeastern University Press, 1995).

28 Review, George Bancroft, "*Specimens of Foreign Standard Literature*. Edited by George Ripley. Vol. III Containing Select Minor Poems, translated from the German of Goethe and Schiller, with Notes. By John S. Dwight. Boston. 1839," *Christian Examiner and General Review* 26, no. 3 (July 1839): 361–78, quotation 361. Cited as Bancroft.

29 Van Wyck Brooks, *The Flowering of New England, 1815–1865* (New York: E. P. Dutton, 1936), 91–92.

30 Review, Cornelius Conway Felton, "*Goethes Werke. Iphigenie auf Tauris. EinS chauspiel* [Goethe's works: Iphegenia in Tauris. A Drama]," *Christian Examiner and General Review* 8 (May 1830): 187–200, quotation 188. Cited as Felton.

31 Bancroft's strong Jacksonian leanings also explain his rancorous assault. He portrayed Goethe as a politically cynical sycophant "who represents the morals, the politics, the imagination, the character, of the broken-down aristocracy." He remained "discreetly silent" on "political subjects" and "adored rank," Bancroft charged, and was "ever ready with flattery for the ruling powers of the day" (Bancroft 363).

32 Margaret Fuller, "Menzel's View of Goethe," *Dial* 1, no. 3 (January 1841): 340–47. Cited as MFMenzel.

33 Margaret Fuller, "Goethe," *Dial* 2, no. 1 (July 1841): 1–41. Cited as MFGoethe.
34 F. J. Stopp, "'Ein Wahrer Narziss': Reflections on the Eduard-Ottilie Relationship in Goethe's *Wahlverwandschaften*," *Publications of the English Goethe Society* 29, n.s. (1959): 71.
35 R. Peacock, "The Ethics of Goethe's *Die Wahlverwandschaften*," *Modern Language Review* 71, no. 2 (April 1976): 340. For a significant dissent to the reading of Ottilie as a representative of Goethe's faith or a figure of innocence, see Walter Benjamin's essay "Goethes *Wahlverwandschaften*" (1924–25), translated by Stanley Corngold in *Walter Benjamin: Selected Writings (1913–1926)*, vol. 1, ed. Marcus Bullock and Michael W. Jennings (Cambridge, MA: Belknap Press of Harvard University Press, 1996), 306–69.
36 N. K. Leacock, "Character, Silence, and the Novel: Walter Benjamin on Goethe's *Elective Affinities*," *Narrative* 10, no. 3 (October 2002): 278.
37 Jeremy Adler, "Goethe's Use of Chemical Theory in His *Elective Affinities*," in *Romanticism and the Sciences*, ed. Andrew Cunningham and Nicholas Jardine (New York: Cambridge University Press, 1990), 263–79, quotations 263, 275.
38 H. Jane Plenderleith "Sex, Lies and *Die Wahlverwandschaften*," *German Life and Letters* 47, no. 4 (1994): 417. Cited as Plenderleith.
39 For a useful survey of the critical response to the novel, see Astride Orle Tantillo, *Goethe's Elective Affinities and the Critics* (Rochester, NY: Camden House, 2001).

Chapter 3

1 For a valuable gathering of essays on transcendentalism and friendship, see John T. Lysaker and William Rossi, eds., *Emerson & Thoreau: Figures of Friendship* (Bloomington: Indiana University Press, 2010).
2 Henry David Thoreau, *A Week on the Concord and Merrimack Rivers* (1849), ed. Carl F. Hovde, William L. Howarth, and Elizabeth H. Witherell (Princeton, NJ: Princeton University Press, 1980).
3 *The Letters of Ralph Waldo Emerson*, ed. Ralph L. Rusk, 6 vols. (New York: Columbia University Press, 1966), 2:168. Cited as *EL*.
4 See also von Mehren 68–69 and Capper 1:277.
5 Jason Hoppe, "'So Much Soul Here I Do Not Need a Book': Idealization and the Aesthetics of Margaret Fuller's Coterie, 1839–1842," *ESQ: A Journal of the American Renaissance* 61, no. 3 (Summer 2015): 363–409.
6 Eleanor M. Tilton "The True Romance of Anna Hazard Barker and Samuel Gray Ward," in *Studies in the American Renaissance, 1987*, ed. Joel Myerson (Charlottesville: University Press of Virginia, 1987), 53–72, quotation 53.
7 On Fuller's traumatic reaction to the Barker-Ward marriage, see Capper 1:279–90 and Marshall 172–83.
8 See also Jeffrey Steele, "Transcendental Friendship: Emerson, Fuller, and Thoreau," in *The Cambridge Companion to Ralph Waldo Emerson*, ed. Joel Porte and Saundra Morris (New York: Cambridge University Press, 1999), 121–39.

9 Robert D. Richardson Jr., *Emerson: The Mind on Fire* (Berkeley: University of California Press, 1995), 328.
10 Kathleen Lawrence, "Soul Sisters and the Sister Arts: Margaret Fuller, Caroline Sturgis, and Their Private World of Love and Art," *ESQ: A Journal of the American Renaissance* 57, no. 1 (2011): 82. For a significant analysis of the Sturgis-Emerson correspondence, see Kathleen Lawrence, "The 'Dry-Lighted Soul': Emerson and His Soul-Mate Caroline Sturgis as Seen in Her Houghton Manuscripts," *Harvard Library Bulletin* 16, no. 3 (Fall 2005): 37–67.
11 Joel Myerson, "Margaret Fuller's 1842 Journal: At Concord with the Emersons," *Harvard Library Journal* 21, no. 3 (1973): 321. Cited as J42.
12 See Marshall 145–47 and Joel Myerson, *The New England Transcendentalists and the Dial* (Cranbury, NJ: Associated University Presses, 1980), 36–42.
13 For a detailed account of Fuller's editorial work for *The Dial*, see Capper 2:3–42 and Joel Myerson, "The *Dial* under Margaret Fuller," the third chapter in *The New England Transcendentalists and the Dial*, 54–76.
14 A. B. Alcott, "Orphic Sayings," *Dial* 1, no. 1 (July 1840): 85–98; A. B. Alcott, "Orphic Sayings," *Dial* 1, no. 3 (July 1841): 351–61; and [James Freeman Clarke], "Art. 13—Orphic Sayings. From Goethe," *Western Messenger* 2 (July 1836): 59–62.
15 Jeffrey Steele, *Transfiguring America: Myth, Ideology, and Mourning in Margaret Fuller's Writing* (Columbia: University of Missouri Press, 2001), 66. Cited as Steele.
16 Dorri Beam, *Style, Gender, and Fantasy in Nineteenth-Century Women's Writing* (Cambridge, UK: Cambridge University Press, 2010), 44. Cited as Beam.
17 E. P. Peabody, "Plan of the West Roxbury Community," *Dial* 2, no. 3 (January 1842): 361–72. For the history of Brook Farm, see Sterling F. Delano, *Brook Farm: The Dark Side of Utopia* (Cambridge, MA: Belknap Press of Harvard University Press, 2004). For an illuminating analysis of the Fourierist theory underlying it, see Richard Francis, *Transcendental Utopias: Individual and Community at Brook Farm, Fruitlands, and Walden* (Ithaca, NY: Cornell University Press, 1997).
18 Albert Brisbane, *Association: Or, A Concise Exposition of the Practical Part of Fourier's Social Science* (New York: Greeley and McElrath, 1843), 40, 3.
19 William Henry Channing, *A Statement of the Principles of the Christian Union* (New York: Press of Hunt's Merchants' Magazine, 1843), 3–4. Cited as CU.
20 Octavius Brooks Frothingham, *Memoir of William Henry Channing* (Boston: Houghton, Mifflin, and Company, 1886), 464–65.
21 William Henry Channing, "Call of the Present.—No. 1—Social Reorganization," *The Present*, October 15, 1843, 42. Cited as *Present*.
22 Margaret Fuller, "The Great Lawsuit. Man *versus* Men. Woman *versus* Women," *Dial* 4, no. 1 (July 1843): 1–47. Cited as GL.
23 Phyllis Cole, "Fuller's Lawsuit and Feminist History," in *Margaret Fuller and Her Circles*, ed. Brigitte Bailey, Katheryn P. Viens, and Conrad Edick Wright (Durham: University of New Hampshire Press, 2013), 13, 14.

24 See Meg McGavran Murray's discussion "Fuller's Apocalypse," in *Margaret Fuller: Wandering Pilgrim* (Athens: University of Georgia Press, 2008), 188–97.
25 For a cogent discussion of this monistic outlook, see Danielle Follett, "The Tension between Immanence and Dualism in Coleridge and Emerson," in *Romanticism and Philosophy: Thinking with Literature*, ed. Sophie Laniel-Musitelli and Thomas Constantinesco (New York: Routledge, 2015), 209–21.
26 Justinus Kerner, *De Seherin von Prevorst* (Stuttgart: Cotta, 1829).
27 Robert D. Habich, "Margaret Fuller's Journal for October 1842," *Harvard Library Bulletin* 33 (Summer 1985): 287, 286.

Chapter 4

1 Margaret Fuller, introduction to *Summer on the Lakes in 1843* (Urbana: University of Illinois Press, 1991), xi.
2 Among the many readings of Fuller's efforts to understand the place of gender in her encounters with Native American women, see Christina Zwarg's explanations of how "Fuller's feminist critique drew direct support from her encounter with the Native Americans" (Zwarg 107); Susan J. Rosowsky's discussion of the "female text" that deepens as *Summer* continues (Rosowsky, 23); and Annette Kolodny's analysis of Fuller's attention to the Chippewa women and the situation of white women (Kolodny 127).
3 *Margaret Fuller: American Romantic*, ed. Perry Miller (New York: Doubleday, 1963), 116. See also Miller's interpretive volume *The Transcendentalists: An Anthology*, ed. Perry Miller (Cambridge, MA: Harvard University Press, 1950).
4 Justinus Kerner, *Die Seherin von Prevorst* (Stuttgart: Cotta, 1829).
5 See John Matteson's astute comment that "Mariana" and *Die Seherin* were "the strongest unifying arcs" of *Summer*, in "Overcoming Fragmentation in *Summer on the Lakes*," *Nineteenth-Century Prose* 42, no. 2 (Fall 2015): 63–92, quotation 86.
6 See Laura Saltz's discussion of the nineteenth-century association of magnetic energy with women in "The Magnetism of a Photograph: Daguerreotypy and Margaret Fuller's Conceptions of Gender and Sexuality," *ESQ* 56 (2nd quarter 2010): 106–34.
7 Mesmerism was a version of the theory of magnetic energy that interested Fuller and many others. See Capper 2:134–36; Cynthia J. Davis, "Margaret Fuller, Body and Soul," *American Literature* 71, no. 1 (March 1999): 31–56; Deborah Manson, "'The Trance of the Ecstatica': Margaret Fuller, Animal Magnetism, and the Transcendent Female Body," *Literature and Medicine* 25, no. 2 (February 2006): 298–324.
8 Alison Winter, "Mesmerism and Popular Culture in Early Victorian England," *History of Science* 32, no. 3 (September 1994): 317–343.
9 Martha L. Berg and Alice de V. Perry, "'The Impulses of Human Nature':

Margaret Fuller's Journal from June through October 1844," *Proceedings of the Massachusetts Historical Society* 102 (1990): 71. Cited as J 1844.

10 For an important discussion of Fuller's friendship with Sturgis, see Kathleen Lawrence, "Soul Sisters and the Sister Arts: Margaret Fuller, Caroline Sturgis, and Their Private World of Love and Art," *ESQ* 57 (2011): 1–2, 79–104.

11 Larry J. Reynolds, "From *Dial* Essay to New York Book: The Making of *Woman in the Nineteenth Century*," in *Periodical Literature in Nineteenth-Century America*, ed. Kenneth M. Price and Susan Belasco Smith (Charlottesville: University of Virginia Press, 1995), 26–27.

12 For further information on Fuller's decision to move to New York, see Capper 2:165–68.

13 On Fuller's retreat to Fishkill Landing, see Capper 2:168–77 and von Mehren 189–99.

14 See von Mehren 189–90; Capper 2:133, 174–75; and Marshall 218–19.

15 See Capper 2:173–76 and Marshall 237–38.

16 Capper 2:197–202.

17 Philip F. Gura, *Man's Better Angels: Romantic Reformers and the Coming of the Civil War* (Cambridge, MA: Belknap Press of Harvard University Press, 2017), 57–98, quotation 74–75.

18 *Margaret Fuller, Critic: Writings from the New-York Tribune, 1844–1846*, ed. Judith Mattson Bean and Joel Myerson (New York: Columbia University Press, 2000), xli. Cited as *MFC*.

19 Barbara Packer, *The Transcendentalists* (Athens: University of Georgia Press, 2007), 205.

20 Ralph Waldo Emerson, "Self-Reliance," *CW* 2:30.

21 For further discussion of Fuller's New York writings, see Marshall 235–43; Capper 2:202–9; Zwarg 189–220; David M. Robinson, "Margaret Fuller, New York, and the Politics of Transcendentalism," *ESQ* 52 (4th quarter 2006): 271–99; and Jeffrey Steele, "Purifying America: Purity and Disability in Margaret Fuller's New York Reform Writing," *ESQ* 52 (4th quarter 2006): 301–17.

Chapter 5

1 Marie Marmo Mullaney, "Feminism, Utopianism and Domesticity: The Career of Rebecca Buffum Spring, 1811–1911," *New Jersey History* 104, no. 3–4 (2002): 1–21.

2 *FL* 4:49, Capper 2:280.

3 Elizabeth Hardwick, "The Genius of Margaret Fuller," *New York Review of Books*, April 10, 1986, 16.

4 See Capper 2:289–91 on Fuller's correspondence with Nathan.

5 Margaret Fuller, *"These Sad but Glorious Days": Dispatches from Europe, 1846–1850*, ed. Larry J. Reynolds and Susan Belasco Smith (New Haven, CT: Yale University Press, 1991), 69. Cited as *SG*.

6 See also Steele 66–69 and 75.
7 On Fuller's self-renewal, see von Mehren 233–36 and Marshall 276–78.
8 See Capper 2:272–73 and 301–5.
9 For details on the school, see SG 100.
10 Von Mehren 240.
11 *The Collected Letters of Thomas and Jane Welsh Carlyle*, ed. C. R. Sanders et al. (Durham, NC: Duke University Press, 1990).
12 Carlyle's letter appeared in *The Times*, June 19, 1844, quoted in Maurizio Masetti, "The 1844 Post Office Scandal and Its Impact on English Public Opinion," in *Exiles, Emigrés and Intermediaries: Anglo-Italian Cultural Transactions*, ed. Barbara Schaff (Amsterdam: Brill, 2010), 205; see also 203–14 for the context and details of the Post Office Scandal event.
13 Giuseppe Mazzini, "Manifesto of Young Italy (1831)," in *A Cosmopolitanism of Nations: Giuseppe Mazzini's Writings on Democracy, Nation Building, and International Relations*, ed. Stefano Recchia and Nadia Urbinati (Princeton, NJ: Princeton University Press, 2009), 33. Cited as Recchia and Urbinati.
14 Recchia and Urbinati, 20.
15 For Mazzini's impact on Fuller's political thinking, see von Mehren 238–40 and Steele 276–78.
16 Charlene Avallone, "Circles Around George Sand: Margaret Fuller and the Dynamics of Transnational Reception," in *Margaret Fuller and Her Circles*, ed. Brigitte Bailey, Katheryn P. Viens, and Conrad Edick Wright (Durham: University of New Hampshire Press, 2013), 208–16. Cited as Avallone.
17 On Fuller's discovery of Sand, see Avallone, 206–28; Gary Williams, "What Did Margaret Think of George?," *Toward a Female Genealogy of Transcendentalism*, ed. Jana L. Argersinger and Phyllis Cole (Athens: University of Georgia Press. 2014), 105–28; and Capper 1:260–62.
18 Giuseppe Mazzini, "George Sand," *Monthly Chronicle* 4 (July 1839): 23–40, quotations 23, 29.
19 See von Mehren 247–49; SG 13–15; Capper 2:316–19; and Ursula Phillips, "Apocalyptic Feminism: Adam Mickiewicz, and Margaret Fuller," *Slavonic and East European Review* 87, no. 1 (January 2009): 1–38. Phillips explains that "on the basis of [Mickiewicz's] letters to Fuller . . . [h]e appears to have been familiar with at least *Woman in the Nineteenth Century*" (4).
20 Larry J. Reynolds, *European Revolutions and the American Literary Renaissance* (New Haven, CT: Yale University Press, 1988), 62.
21 Leona Rostenberg, "Mazzini to Margaret Fuller, 1847–1849," *American Historical Review* 47 (October 1941): 76.
22 Since no document or other legal evidence of this marriage was found after her death, Fuller's marriage became an enigmatic issue in her extensive biographical record. See Capper 2:365–70; Marshall 355–58; and Joan von Mehren, "Margaret Fuller, the Marchese Giovanni Ossoli, and the Marriage Question: Considering

the Research of Dr. Roberto Colzi," *Resources for American Literary Study* 30 (2005): 104–43.

23 On Garibaldi's efforts to protect Rome, see Capper 2:448–58. Fuller described Garibaldi's powerful retreat as "worthy of the pen of Xenophon" (SG 314).

24 Larry J. Reynolds, *Righteous Violence: Revolution, Slavery, and the American Renaissance* (Athens: University of Georgia Press, 2011), 38. Cited as *RV*.

25 Barbara L. Packer, *The Transcendentalists* (Athens: University of Georgia Press, 2007), 216.

26 See Julia Ward Howe, *Margaret Fuller (Marchesa Ossoli)* (Boston: Roberts Brothers, 1883); and Thomas Wentworth Higginson, *Margaret Fuller Ossoli* (Boston: Houghton, 1884).

INDEX

abolitionism, 126, 135
abolitionists, 97, 109
Adler, Jeremy, 51
Alcott, Amos Bronson, 36, 42–43; "Orphic Sayings," 68
Allston, Washington, 141n20
America: failures of, 125–26; politics of, 130
American Monthly Magazine, 34
American nation, fate of, 91
Americans: intellectual complacency of, 35; utilitarianism of, 35–36
"Annus Mirabilis" compositions, 34
antislavery movement. *See also* abolitionists, 79, 97, 109, 135
anti-transcendentalism, 8, 47
Associationism, 74–76, 97, 109
Asylum for the Insane, 106
Austen, Jane, 41
Austria, 114–15, 122–23, 128–29
Avallone, Charlene, 116

Bancroft, George, 46–47, 49
Barker, Anna, 18, 32, 57–58, 60–61, 64, 80, 82–83, 90, 96, 109
Barker, Elizabeth, 138n17
Bartram, Harry, 28

Beam, Dorri, 69
Bean, Judith Mattson, 103
Beecher Stowe, Harriet, 41
Beethoven, Ludwig van, 39–40
Belasco, Susan, 2, 86
Bellevue Alms House, 106
Ben Lomond, Scottish Highlands, 111, 113
Berg, Martha, 95
Blackwell's Island Penitentiary, 106–7
Blanchard, Paula, 21
Boston, Massachusetts, 4–5; antislavery movement in, 97; Fuller as presence on literary scene in, 40–41; Unitarianism in, 4–6
Brisbane, Albert, 75–76, 108; *Association*, 74
British Museum, 114
Brook Farm, 74–75, 77, 98
Brooks, Van Wyck, 47
Brown, John, 109
Browning, Elizabeth Barrett, 41
Bruce, Georgiana, 98, 101
Buffum, Arthur, 109

Calvinism, Unitarianism's departure from, 4–6
Calvinists, Puritan, 4

Cambridge, Massachusetts, 4–5, 12, 18–20, 30, 67, 96–97
Capper, Charles, 1–2, 19, 30–31, 55, 69, 73, 134
Carlyle, Jane Welsh, 41, 114
Carlyle, Thomas, 13–15, 114–15
Cervantes, Miguel de, 27
Channing, William Ellery, 5–6, 75
Channing, William Henry, 5, 22, 67, 98, 101–2; Associationism and, 75–76, 94–95, 97, 108–9; correspondence with, 76–77, 94; Emerson and, 75–76; "Ernest the Seeker," 68; "Social Reorganization," 76
Chevigny, Bell Gale, 1, 60
Child, Lydia Maria, 103
Chippewa, 87
Christian Examiner, 46, 66–67
Christianity, 11–13, 37, 88, 94
Christian Union of Associationists, 75, 94
Clarke, James Freeman, 6–7, 22, 29, 31, 34–35, 95; aspirations for ministry, 17–18; Coleridge and, 7–8, 13–14; correspondence with, 9–12, 16, 30–33; friendship with, 3–5; launches *The Western Messenger*, 66–67; in Louisville, Kentucky, 20; self-discovery and, 8–9; tour of American frontier and, 85; transcendentalism and, 7–8; translation of Goethe's poems as "Orphic Sayings," 68
Clarke, Sarah Ann, 85
Clarke, William, 95–96
Clarkson, Thomas, 97
Cole, Phyllis, 45, 78
Coleridge, Samuel Taylor, 7–9, 13; *Aids to Reflection*, 8, 138n8; *The Friend*, 10–11
Concord, 31, 97, 117
"Concord circle," 31
consciousness, 8, 28, 40
Conversations, 42–46, 55–56, 116, 141n20
conversation(s), 11–16, 42; feminist agency and, 41; Fuller's quest for, 56–57; lack of, 20. *See also* dialogue, search for

the "Daimonic," 39–40
Davis, George, 11–12
democracy, idea of, 2, 125–26, 129, 131, 133–35
democratic theory, 114
The Dial, 31, 46–47, 49–50, 66–68, 74, 77–78, 85, 102
dialogue, search for, 17, 43–45
dreams, 9
dualism, 83
duty, idea of, 38
Dwight, John Sullivan, 68; *Select Minor Poems of Goethe and Schiller*, 46

Eckermann, Johan Peter, 39–40; *Conversations with Goethe*, 36–37, 40–43, 46, 67
Edinburgh, Scotland, 111–12
education, 19, 101
Eichhorn, Gottfried, 12
electricity, 93–94
the *Elizabeth*, 134
Emerson, Charles, 68
Emerson, Lidian, 65
Emerson, Ralph Waldo, 1, 3–5, 13–15, 18, 22, 30–31, 38, 42–43, 60, 68, 97, 118, 138n17; Channing and, 75–76; *The Dial* and, 67; friendship with Fuller, 34–35, 55–59, 61–67, 80, 104–5, 124–25, 126–27, 132–33; philosophy of, 105–6; the soul and, 81–82; as spokesman for transcendentalism, 55; takes over editorship of *The Dial*, 77–78; women's rights and, 45. *See also* Emerson, Ralph Waldo, works of
Emerson, Ralph Waldo, works of: "Circles," 57; "Divinity School Address," 36, 75–76; "Emancipation in the British West Indies," 97; *Essays: First Series*, 57; *Essays: Second Series*, 103–5; "Experience," 104; lectures on the "Present Age," 45; *Nature*, 24, 34; "The Oversoul," 81; "The Poet," 104; "Self-Reliance," 56, 57, 99, 100–101; "Threnody," 66
Emerson, Waldo, 65–66, 104
Europe, 107, 109; desire to see and know, 17–18, 32–34; dispatches from, 2, 111–13, 122–23, 128–30, 133–35; travel to, 103, 108–35. *See also specific locations*

European literature, 18. *See also* German literature; *specific authors*
Eustis, William, 68

Farm School, 106
Farnham, Eliza, 98, 103
Farrar, Eliza, 18–20, 32–34, 41–42, 59–60, 138n17; *The Young Lady's Friend*, 18–19
Farrar, John, 33, 138n17
Felton, Cornelius Conway, 46–49
female domestic sphere, 44
female intellectuals, 41
"femality," 82
feminism, 43–45, 89, 93. *See also* women's liberation
feminist agency, 41
Fishkill Landing, New York, 96
Florence, Italy, 125, 133
flowers, 26–27, 68–71
Fourier, Charles, 57, 74–76, 99, 102–3
Fourierism, 74–75, 95
Fourierist convention, 108–9
Fourierists, 102–3, 108–9
France, 124, 126, 129, 131–34
Freeman, James, 6–7
friendship circle, 57–61, 63–65, 82–83; engagement with, 93; loss of, 80, 90, 95–96, 109
friendship(s), 9–11, 16, 28, 55–84; friendship circle, 57–61, 63–65, 80, 82–83, 90, 93, 95–96, 109; philosophy and, 16; spiritual unions in, 96; transcendentalism's discourse on, 64. *See also specific friends*
Fuller, Ellen, 120
Fuller, Margaret, 133, 135; arrival in London, 114–15; "art of," 2; asks for literature of engagement and interaction, 38–39; aspires to write first biography of Goethe in English, 32–33; becomes head of Fuller household, 21, 29–30; biography of, 19, 22; breaks with Springs, 120–21; childhood of, 25–27; Conversations and, 42–46, 55–56, 116, 141n20; as cultural critic, 103–4, 106–7; dazzling prose of, 62–63; death of, 134; defense of Goethe, 36–37, 46–51; desire to see and know Europe, 17–18, 32–34; disappointment with America's failures, 125–26; doubts about Christian revelation, 11–13; editorship of *The Dial*, 46–47, 66–68, 74, 77–78, 85, 102; embraces transitive, metamorphic God, 37–38; Emerson and, 34–35, 55–59, 61–66, 80, 104–5, 124–27, 132–33; in Europe, 103; experimentation in literary forms, 68; family moves to Groton, 19–20; financial crisis and, 21, 29, 32–33; in Groton, Massachusetts, 20–21, 29–32, 55; haunted by ungratefulness, 21; health issues of, 21, 93–94; intention to bring an awakening, 44–45; isolation of, 20–21, 30, 32, 55, 95; joins war effort in Italy, 131–32; as key figure in "New Era" of progressive politics, 135; life's mission, 2; literary aspirations of, 17–19, 32–33; literary contribution to transcendentalist movement, 34; as literary editor for *New-York Tribune*, 103–6, 108–9; loneliness of, 26–27, 30, 61; love of nature, 26–27; meets George Sand, 116–18; mother of, 21, 26; moves to New York, 96–97, 102–3, 108; in Paris, France, 117–18; pregnancy of, 126–28; as presence on Boston literary scene, 40–41; as progressive spokeswoman, 116; redirection in early 1840s, 64; rediscovery of, 1–2; relationship with her father, 20–21, 48; relationship with Sturgis, 63–65; romantic fixation on Ward, 59–61; self-remaking of, 66–67; the soul and, 81–82; teaching at Greene Street School, Providence, 55; on tour of American frontier, 85–88, 97; translation of Eckermann's *Conversation with Goethe*, 36, 40–41, 67; translation of Goethe's *Tasso*, 31–32, 34; trip to Europe, 107–35; tutors younger siblings, 20–21; Unitarian ethos of self-culture, 19; urge for reformism, 76–77; virginity of, 119; visits Emerson family, 65–66; *Woman in the Nineteenth*

Fuller, Margaret (*continued*)
Century, 1–2, 56–57, 63, 96–98, 100, 102, 104, 119, 121; work with imprisoned women, 98, 101, 116. *See also* Fuller, Margaret, works of

Fuller, Margaret, works of: article on Mazzini for *Tribune*, 114; "Autobiographical Romance," 22–29, 80; dispatches from Europe to *Tribune*, 2, 111–13, 122–23, 128–30, 133–35; essay on *Die Seherin von Prevorst*, 92; essays on Italy for *Tribune*, 122–23; "Goethe," 49–50; "The Great Lawsuit," 77–86, 90, 92–93, 95, 97, 98–99, 104; journals of, 56–57, 62–63, 65–66, 82–83, 86, 95–96; "Leila," 73–74; letters of, 2, 34, 56–57, 60, 62–65, 76–77, 109–10, 121–22 (*see also specific correspondents*); "Lost on Ben Lomond," 112; "The Magnolia of Lake Pontchartrain," 68–72; "Mariana," 89–92; "Our City Charities," 106; "Present State of German Literature," 34–37; "Reading Journal O," 42; review of biography of Tasso for *The Dial*, 31–32; review of Emerson for *Tribune*, 104–6; self-portrait in "The Great Lawsuit," 79–80; *Summer on the Lakes*, 82, 86, 88–91, 93, 95; translation of and preface to *Eckermann's Conversations with Goethe*, 36–37, 40–43, 46, 67; translation of Eckermann's *Conversation with Goethe*, 42–43, 55; writing for *New-York Tribune*, 95–96, 102–4; "Yuca Filamentosa," 71–73

Fuller, Timothy, 19, 48, 80; death of, 21–22, 29, 32, 61; father of, 23; Jeffersonianism of, 19; Margaret's portrait of, 22–26

Fuller scholarship, revisionist, 89

Gaeta, Italy, 130
gardens, 26–27
Garibaldi, Giuseppe, 131
gender, 25–26, 96, 100
German, study of, 3–4, 12, 31, 34, 46
German biblical criticism, 5–6
Germanic studies, 33–35
German literature, 3–4, 12–15, 17–18, 20, 29–36, 46–48, 60, 67, 69, 92, 98–99
German philosophy, 14–16, 31, 33–35

German romanticism, 13–14
Germany, 120
Goethe, Johann Wolfgang von, 15, 17–18, 20, 29–31, 35–36, 40, 96, 98–99, 120; appreciation of, 47–52; attacks on, 46–51; conception of the "Daimonic," 39–40; Conversation group about, 42–43; cosmopolitan freedom of, 37, 38–39, 48, 105; Fuller's ambition to write first biography of in English, 32–33; Fuller's defense of, 36–37, 46–50; intellectual independence of, 37; on marriage, 52; portrayal of self-subsistent women, 100; reputation under attack by New England clergy, 36–37; translation of, 31–32, 34; in Weimar, 33. *See also* Goethe, Johann Wolfgang von, works of

Goethe, Johann Wolfgang von, works of: *Elective Affinities*, 3, 38, 47, 49–55; *Faust*, 3; "The Godlike," 48; *Hermann and Dorothea*, 3; *Iphegenia*, 3; *Memoirs*, 3; *The Sorrows of Young Werther*, 51, 141n20; *Tasso*, 3, 31–32, 34

Graham, James, 115
Great Britain, 114
Greek mythology, 26
Greeley, Horace, 95–96, 102–3, 108–9, 134
Greene Street School, 42, 55
Groton, Massachusetts, 12, 19–21, 29–30, 32, 55, 89
Gura, Philip, 102–3

Hardwick, Elizabeth, 110
Harring, Harro, *Dolores: A Novel of South America*, 113
Hartley, David, 6–7, 9
Harvard College, 12
Harvard University, 4, 29, 46–47; Harvard Divinity School, 12; Harvard University libraries, 2, 42, 86, 95; Houghton Library, 42; Unitarianism and, 5
Hauffe, Frederica, 89, 92, 94
Hawthorne, Nathaniel, 106
Hedge, Frederic Henry, 5, 8–9, 12–13, 29, 31, 34–36, 46, 66–67
Higginson, Thomas Wentworth, 18, 21, 135

Hoar, Elizabeth, 117, 142n22
Hoppe, Jason, 60
Howe, Julia Ward, 135
Hudson River, 96
Hudspeth, Robert N., 2, 34, 109–10, 128
Humboldt, Wilhelm von, 46

Idealism, 14
imagination, 9
individualism, 75–76
inner awareness, 8–9
intellectual growth, 11
Italian Gratuitous School, 113
Italy, 113, 119–33; emancipation of, 97, 114, 116, 122; war effort in, 131–32

Kant, Immanuel, 7, 13–14
Kantian idealism, 8
Kantianism, 7–8, 15
Kerner, Justinus, 92–94; *Die Seherin von Prevorst (Seeress of Prevorst)*, 82, 89
Kilshaw, Ellen, 18, 27–28
Kimball, J. Horace, 97
King's Chapel, 6

L'Aquila, Italy, 127
Latin, study of, 3
Lawrence, Kathleen, 64–65
learning, as dialogic process, 20
Lincoln, Abraham, 91
literature, 67; as entry to life, not substitute for it, 40; transcendentalism and, 67. *See also* German literature; *specific authors*
Loch Katrine, Scotland, 111
Locke, John, 6–7
Longfellow, Henry Wadsworth, 106
Louis Philippe, dethronement of, 129
Louisville, Kentucky, 67
love, the mystical and, 15

Mackinaw Island, 87
magnetism, 92–93
male public sphere, 44
marriage, 52, 80–81, 90–91
Marsh, James, 8, 138n8
Marshall, Megan, 2, 22, 95–96, 118, 131

Martineau, Harriet, 138n17
Massachusetts Historical Society, 2
Mazzini, Giuseppe, 107, 113–17, 119–20, 124–25, 131, 133; "Manifesto to Young Italy," 115; "Nationalism and Cosmopolitanism," 116; political vision of, 115–16; on Sand, 117
Mehren, Joan von, 18, 128
Menzel, Wolfgang, 46–48
Mesmer, Anton, 93–94
mesmerism, 93–94
metaphysics, 15
Mickiewicz, Adam, 107, 118–21
Miller, Perry, 88–89; "Annus Mirabilis" compositions, 34
mind, nature of, 9
mind-body duality, 94
Miss Preston's School, 89
Moers, Ellen, 41
Molière (Jean-Baptiste Poquelin), 27
moon, 72–73, 112
music, 40
Myerson, Joel, 2, 65, 103

Nathan, James, 109–10, 113
Native people: Americans' disdain for, 87–88; displacement of, 88; exploitation of, 86, 88; grim condition of, 86–87; mistreatment of, 97; Native women, 87–88. *See also specific peoples*
New England Anti-Slavery Society, 109
New England Unitarianism. *See also* Unitarianism
"newness," allegiance to, 4–5
New York, 96–97, 102–3, 106–8
New-York Tribune, 95–96, 102–109, 116; article on Mazzini for, 114; contributions to, 2; essays on Italy for *Tribune*, 122–23; Fuller's dispatches from Europe to *Tribune*, 2, 111–13, 122–23, 128–30, 133–35
Niagara Falls, 86–87
Norton, Andrews, 5–6, 36–37
Novalis (Georg Philipp Friedrich Freiherr von Hardenberg), 4, 13–15, 17–18, 35, 81, 94

Ossoli, Angelo Eugene Philip (Nino), 128, 134
Ossoli, Giovanni Angelo, 120, 122, 127–28, 131–34
Ottawa, 87

Packer, Barbara, 14, 103–4, 134
Panic of 1837, 103
Papal States, 122–23
Paris, France, 117–18, 121
Parker, Theodore, 68
paternal authority, 19–21, 22
Peabody, Elizabeth Palmer, 34, 42, 44–45, 142n22; "Plan of the West Roxbury Community," 74–75
perceptions, 8–9, 82, 112
Perry, Alice, 95
philosophy: friendship and, 16; German, 14–16, 31, 33–35. *See also specific philosophers*
Pius IX, Pope, 122–25, 128–31
Poe, Edgar Allan, 106
"poetics of resistance," 22
poetry, transcendentalism and, 67
Polk, James K., 46
Post Office Scandal, 114–15
The Present, 76
prison reform, 106–7, 109
Providence, Rhode Island, 42, 55
provincialism, American, 37
Puritanism, 4–5

Quakers, 109

Reason, 7–9
reformism, 97, 103, 109; coverage of, 103; transcendentalism and, 104–5; urge for, 76–77
relationships: self-making, 28. *See also* friendship(s)
religion, 11–13. *See also* Christianity; Unitarianism; spirituality
revolution(s), 107, 113, 115, 124, 128–29, 131–32, 134–35
Reynolds, Larry J., 2, 96, 122, 133
Richardson, Robert D., 64

Rieti, Italy, 127, 130
Ripley, George, 36, 66–67, 74, 77; Specimens of Foreign Standard Literature series, 46–47
Ripley, Sophia, 42–44
Ritchie, Amanda, 42, 141n20
Rome, Italy, 119–20, 122–24, 126–35
Rossi, Pellegrino, 130–31

Saint-Simonianism, 116
salons, 41–42
Sand, George, 41, 81, 116–18
Schiller, Friedrich, 4, 46–47
Schleiermacher, Friedrich, 46
Scott, Walter, 27
the séance, 93
Sedgwick, Catharine, 103
the self, narrated, 22
self-awareness, 29
self-construction, 27
self-culture, Unitarian ethos of, 19
self-deception, 61
self-development, 19, 42, 45, 99
self-disapproval, 22
self-discovery, 7–9
self-expression, 20, 45, 87
selfhood, 88
"self-impulse," 100
self-knowledge, 116
self-possession, 98–99
self-reconstruction, 55–56
self-reflection, 16, 22
self-reliance, 11–12, 98–100, 112
self-renewal, 113
self-respect, 116
self-revelatory writing, 22
self-sacrifice, 38
self-subsistence, 98–99
self-writing, women and, 22
sensation, 8–9
sexuality, 96
Shakespeare, William, 27; *Romeo and Juliet*, 26
Simmons, Nancy Craig, 44–45, 142n22
Sing Sing prison, 98
skepticism, 11–13

slavery, 76, 101–2, 125–26, 130; abolition of, 97; antislavery movement, 79, 97, 109, 126, 135. *See also* abolitionists
Smith, Sidonie, 22
social injustice, 80, 106
socialism, 94, 134
the soul, 81–82, 101; monistic, 81–83
the South, 101–2
spiritual ecstasy, 93
spirituality, 72–73, 94
Spring, Eddie, 109–12
Spring, Marcus, 108–12, 118, 120–21
Spring, Rebecca Buffum, 108–12, 118–22
Staël, Germaine de, 41; *Corinne; or Italy*, 41, 43; *Germany*, 41; influence on Fuller, 41
Steele, Jeffrey, 69, 73, 106, 112
Sturgis, Caroline, 56–58, 60, 62, 64–65, 67, 95–97, 126–27
subjugation, 97; racial, 89; of women, 89
Swedenborg, Emanuel, 99
Switzerland, 120, 124

Tappan, Caroline Sturgis. *See* Sturgis, Caroline
Tasso, Torquato, 31–32
Temple School, 36, 42
Thoreau, Henry David, 1; essays for *The Dial*, 68; *A Week on the Concord and Merrimack Rivers*, 56
Thorne, James A., 97
Ticknor, George, 141n20
Tilton, Eleanor M., 60–61
The Times, 115
Towianski, Andrew, 118
Transcendental Club, 67
Transcendental Controversy, 36
transcendentalism, 1, 5–6, 14–15, 24, 36–37, 47, 64–65, 99, 107; "Annus Mirabilis" compositions, 34; Associationism and, 74–76; Coleridge's contribution to, 7–8; darker version of, 24–25; *The Dial* and, 66–68; Emerson as spokesman for, 55; Fuller as public voice of, 66–67; individualism and, 75–76; literature and, 67; poetry and, 67; reformism and, 104–5
transcendentalists. *See also specific transcendentalists*, 10, 14, 42, 89, 97
travel narratives, 88; dispatches from, 2, 111–13, 122–23, 128–30, 133–35
Trivulzio di Belgioioso, Cristina, 131–32

Understanding, 7–8
Unitarian clergy, 4–5, 35
Unitarianism, 6–7, 66, 75; beginnings of, 5; ethos of self-culture, 19; two faces of, 5–6
utilitarianism, 35–36

Venice, 120
"vibratiuncles," 7
Vulpius, Christiane, 37

Ward, Samuel Gray, 18, 32, 57–61, 64, 67, 80, 90, 96, 109, 138n17
Weimar, Germany, 47
Western Messenger, 66–68
West Street Book Shop, 42
Whig Party, 102–3
Wieland, Christoph Martin, 47
Wilson, William Dexter, 67–68
Winters, Alison, 93
Wollstonecraft, Mary, 81
women: domestic sphere and, 44; education of, 101; imprisoned, 98, 101, 116; self-development and, 19, 41; self-writing and, 22; subjugation of, 53–55, 85, 87, 97, 117. *See also* women's equality, theory of; women's liberation
women's equality, theory of, racial implications of, 101–2
women's liberation, 1, 19, 29, 40–45, 77–86, 88, 94, 99, 100–1, 114, 116
women's rights. *See* women's liberation

Zwarg, Christina, 31, 41, 57, 62, 93

DAVID ROBINSON was born and raised in Odessa, Texas and was educated at the University of Texas, Harvard Divinity School, and the University of Wisconsin. He now resides with his wife in Corvallis, Oregon, where he is an Emeritus Professor of English at Oregon State University. During his academic career he was chosen for a chaired position as the Oregon Professor of English and was also named a Distinguished Professor at the University. For several years he was the Director of the Center for the Humanities at OSU. He is the author of many articles, papers, and books, including *Apostle of Culture: Emerson as a Preacher and Lecturer* (1982), *The Unitarians and the Universalists* (1985), *Emerson and the Conduct of Life* (1993), *World of Relations: The Achievement of Peter Taylor* (1998), and *Natural Life: Thoreau's Worldly Transcendentalism* (2004).

www.ingramcontent.com/pod-product-compliance
Lightning Source LLC
Chambersburg PA
CBHW031834230426
43669CB00009B/1351